THE MASTERPIECES
GUIDE

ENGLISH

Marleen Dominicus - van Soest

THE MASTERPIECES
GUIDE

CONTENTS

PREFACE

Visitors come from all over the world to admire the collections in the Rijksmuseum. For most of them the main attraction is Dutch painting of the 17th century, known as the Golden Age. The broad range of great works by Rembrandt, Frans Hals, Jacob van Ruisdael, Jan Steen and Joannes Vermeer ensure that nowhere else can the special character and high quality of the Dutch school of painting be appreciated so well.

The Rijksmuseum was founded in 1798 and opened its doors to the public in 1800. At that time it was located in part of Huis ten Bosch in The Hague, the present palace of H.M. Queen Beatrix. Eight years later, King Louis Bonaparte, Napoleon's brother, moved the Rijksmuseum to Amsterdam, and added to the collection Rembrandt's 'Night Watch', which was owned by the City of Amsterdam, as well as other works. In 1885 the museum moved into the richly ornamented building designed by the architect Pierre Cuypers, which has been an Amsterdam landmark ever since. Together with the Stedelijk Museum, the Van Gogh Museum and the Concertgebouw, the Rijksmuseum now forms the heart of the city museums, around the Museumplein.

In the next few years the Rijksmuseum is to undergo a far-reaching renovation programme. For the first time in the more than 100 years of its existence the whole of Cuypers' building will be restored to its former glory. In 2000 the Dutch government provided an initial amount of 45 million euro as a millennium gift and since then Royal Philips Electronics as founder, and the BankGiro Lottery and ING as chief sponsors, have made substantial donations. In gratitude for this, the southern wing of the museum, where *Rijksmuseum The Masterpieces* are now on display, has been renamed the Philips Wing. The Rijksmuseum has more than a million works of art and historical objects in its collection. The period covered is 1400 to 1900, which will be extended into the 20th century after the renovations. While Cuypers' main building is being renovated, however, the Rijksmuseum is concentrating exclusively on the art and history of the Golden Age. Under the title *Rijksmuseum The Masterpieces* the very finest of what Holland produced in the 17th century is on view. In the first place, of course, this means the paintings by the great masters, but there is more than that. The unique dolls houses, an impressive ship's model and the world-famous delftware are also displayed. What makes a visit to the Rijksmuseum so special is that sculpture, the decorative arts and the history of the 17th century are also presented to the highest standards. More than two centuries of collecting have resulted in the most wide-ranging and representative survey of art in what was then the Republic of the United Provinces.

With its strong fleet and worldwide trading ventures, the Netherlands in the 17th century was a formidable power which commanded the respect of other countries in Europe. In the Dutch East India Company (VOC) the Republic created what was in essence the first multinational. Prosperity and flourishing arts went hand in hand. The spirit of enterprise was combined with curiosity, so that science too made rapid strides. Moreover, tolerance ensured that many who feared for their safety or religious freedom elsewhere found a welcome in the Netherlands. This unique story will be presented in the Philips Wing of the Rijksmuseum in the years ahead. A masterly experience awaits you!

Wim Pijbes
Director General of the Rijksmuseum

INTRODUCTION

THE MIRACLE OF THE GOLDEN AGE

In the 17th century the Netherlands prospered as never before. Later on this period became known as the Golden Age. The Netherlands was then one of the richest countries in the world, a great power with a flourishing culture. The level of prosperity, even for ordinary folk, the freedom and the far-reaching equality made a deep impression on people in the neighbouring countries. They were amazed because the Netherlands was a republic, ruled by its citizens, whereas their own countries were ruled by kings or princes, and because the small country proved able to hold its own in Europe. The Netherlands was thought to be a miracle.

'Scarce any subject occurs more frequent in the discourses of ingenious men than that of the marvellous progress of this little state which, in the space of about hundreds years ... hath grown to a height, not only infinitely transcending all the ancient republics of Greece, but not much inferior in some respects even to the greatest monarchies of these latter ages,' William Aglionby, an Englishman, declared admiringly in 1669. William Temple was equally-plain spoken: the Netherlands was 'the envy of some, the fear of others, and the wonder of all neighbours'. This pithy view was expressed in 1673, when the country was at war with three of its neighbours.

REPUBLIC

What was extraordinary about the dynamic development of the Republic of the Seven United Provinces, as the country was officially known, was that it took place at a time of great political uncertainty. In the 16th century the seven Dutch provinces that were to form the Republic were still part, together with ten other provinces, of a larger area which roughly contained the modern countries of the Netherlands, Belgium and Luxembourg. The seventeen Netherlands provinces belonged to the empire of the King of Spain, Philip II.

The Netherlands rebelled against his pro-Catholic and centralising policy in 1568. This revolt led eventually to the separation of North and South, the areas which now more or less form the Netherlands and Belgium, and of Protestants and Catholics. In 1581 a large number of provinces renounced the Spanish king. The Northern provinces united in an independent federation in 1588: this was the Republic of the Seven United Provinces. Its highest authority was not a sovereign but a body of citizens drawn from the representatives of the seven provinces, the States General.

In each province the function of stadholder, a sort of governor, which already existed under the Spanish, was retained. The stadholder stood at the head of the army and the navy, but formally he was in the service of one province. Some provinces had the same stadholder. The post was always filled by sons and nephews of William of Orange, the first leader of the revolt, and their descendants. Meantime the war against Spain continued. The peace treaty was not signed until 1648, after eighty years of war. The Dutch Republic was not officially recognised until then.

IMMIGRANTS

An important event in the development of the young state was the capture by the Spanish of the port of Antwerp in the Southern Netherlands in 1585 and the subsequent blockade of the River Scheldt by the rebels. Thousands of merchants in the Southern Netherlands fled to the North, which was now liberated from the Spanish, taking with them their money, their expertise and their business connections. In their wake came entrepreneurs, craftsmen and artists, often for religious reasons but also simply to earn money. They settled chiefly in the coastal areas, in cities such as Haarlem, Delft, Leiden and Amsterdam and Middelburg. This marked the beginning of a period of unprecedented growth. Haarlem and Leiden became important centres of the textile industry, producing linen in the case of Haarlem and laken (a woollen fabric) in the case of Leiden. Delft became famous for its carpets and high-quality earthenware.

But most spectacular of all was the development of Amsterdam. At the end of the 16th century the city began to grow rapidly, from a population of 30,000 in 1585 to 50,000 in 1600. Amsterdam soon became a trade centre with a worldwide reputation where goods from all over the globe were bought and sold. Attracted by this prosperity, more and more people moved to the city: in 1640 the population was 140,000 and in 1700 220,000. Amsterdam's astonishing growth and affluence are reflected in the belt of canals built round the old centre and the new town hall on the Dam.

TRADE AND SHIPPING

'Our greatest strength and prosperity consists in the Imperium maris [rule of the sea] and in foreign commerce.' True words, spoken at the beginning of the 17th century by the Amsterdam burgomaster and merchant C.P. Hooft. These were indeed the factors underlying the success of the Dutch Republic. To the existing Baltic trade was now added trade with the Mediterranean and, taking a lead from Spain and Portugal, with Asia and America. The last of these provided opportunities for telling blows against the Spanish, the enemy until the peace of 1648.
In order to combine the operations of the merchants, two trading organisations were set up, the Dutch East India Company (VOC) in 1602 and the West India Company in 1621. Shares were issued which anyone could buy and they were snapped up, not only by rich investors but by servants and artists. The engraver Jan Saenredam put no less than 2400 guilders into the VOC, a substantial sum equal to seven times a worker's annual pay. It proved to be a shrewd investment. The annual dividend was sometimes 40% of the nominal value. This provided a reliable source of income for Jan's son, the painter Pieter Saenredam. A spirit of enterprise, efficient management, soundly built ships and capable seamen guaranteed the success of the Dutch merchant fleet. In 1629 Amsterdam merchants contentedly concluded that they had driven all nations 'out of the water'. Until late in the 17th century the Netherlands controlled most of the European cargo trade and also dominated the world's seas. William Temple, who was the English envoy in The Hague from 1668 to 1673, confirmed this in 1673. According to him, no land could be found, in the present or in historical documents, with such an extensive trade network.

RICH IN CULTURE

Trade and industry were concentrated in the cities. There the riches were earned. This is still evident today when one walks through the centre of Amsterdam with its imposing canal mansions and town hall. They bear witness to the flourishing culture of the Golden Age. But architecture is only one facet; the culture was infinitely rich and diverse. Literature, theatre, book printing, painting, decorative arts, philosophy, technology and science were all on the highest level. Huygens, Vondel, Grotius, Stevin, Leeghwater, Leeuwenhoek, Rembrandt, Spinoza are some of the names that testify to this.
Of all these fields painting nearly always made the most impression. The Englishman Peter Mundy was far from being the only 17th-century observer to note that the Dutch had a great love of paintings. They were to be found in every house, expensive pieces among the rich and cheaper ones at the baker's or the butcher's. Even smiths and cobblers had some sort of painting in their workshop. It is estimated that in the Golden Age 5 million paintings were made, probably even more. This had to do with the rise, after 1580, of a very comfortably-off middle class who set about decorating their homes in imitation of the rich. To meet the demand and to cater for differing tastes, new ways of working were sought. They were found in specialisation, standardisation and greater productivity. The result was a wide range of new genres, in which quality was variable. Hundreds of artists moved to the Republic to try their luck. Amsterdam in particular, with its international trading contacts, worked like a magnet.
In the second half of the 17th century the demand for paintings gradually decreased. The market was oversupplied and other art forms – silver, furniture, landscape architecture – came into fashion. The wars against England, and in 1672 with France and Germany too, cost a great deal. This last war had an especially disastrous effect on the art market. Many artists could no longer make ends meet and were forced to choose another profession.

REPUBLIC AND WORLD POWER

GOLDEN AGE

The 17th century was a Golden Age for the Netherlands. Despite waging war almost continuously, the small country on the North Sea became a powerful and prosperous state where the arts flourished. Trade and shipping were the main generators of wealth. The port of Amsterdam was the centre of world trade and the Dutch and their ships were to be found all over the globe.

The Netherlands, moreover, was different from all other countries. It was a republic governed by its citizens, whereas the neighbouring lands were ruled by kings. The hard-won freedom of the young country was a source of pride to its people, but it had to be continually defended.

• pages 10-17

REPUBLIC

In the Republic of the Seven United Provinces power was in the hands of the citizens. The highest authority was entrusted to the representatives of the seven provinces, the States General. They convened in The Hague.

The legal advisors of the provinces, known as pensionaries, had high positions. The provinces were autonomous in many fields and had their own States. Holland was the most powerful province and Protestantism the dominant faith. There were regular clashes with the Prince of Orange. He was appointed stadholder (a sort of governor) by the provincial States and was supreme commander of the army and the fleet.

• pages 24-27; 30-33

NAVAL POWER

The economic success of the Republic was due in large part to the strength of the fleet. Not only did it have more ships than any other European nation, it also had outstanding naval commanders. Maarten Tromp and Michiel de Ruyter were internationally famous and worshipped as heroes in their native country.

But as a sea-faring nation, the Republic was also vulnerable. There were always rivals lying in wait. After 1650 England became the main competitor at sea, and the two countries fought three naval wars.

• pages 18-23

THE STRUGGLE FOR 'TRUE LIBERTY'

The years 1618-1619 are a black page in the history of the young Republic. In the summer of 1618 the political and religious conflicts between the nation's two successful leaders, stadholder Maurice and pensionary Johan van Oldenbarnevelt, escalated. The 71-year-old Van Oldenbarnevelt, the brilliant jurist Grotius and other sympathizers who supported the principle of a free republic and feared the growing power of the stadholder were arrested and condemned after long and dubious trials. Grotius was sentenced to life imprisonment and Van Oldenbarnevelt to death.

• pages 28-29

THE NETHERLANDS AND THE WORLD

At the end of the 16th century the first Dutch ships ventured beyond Europe. They set course for Asia, Africa and America in search of trade. To coordinate the efforts of the various merchants, two trade organizations were founded: the Dutch East India Company or VOC and the West India Company or WIC.

The VOC, established in 1602, traded with Asia and quickly became the world's biggest trade and transport enterprise, with branches in Africa and many Asian countries. The WIC, established in 1621, traded with West Africa and America.

• pages 34-41

BARTHOLOMEUS

A group of civic guards in Amsterdam are holding a banquet to mark the end of the Eighty Years War with Spain. The Peace of Münster, concluded on 15 May 1648, meant official recognition for the Dutch Republic. Independence had come at last.

The poem behind the drum's snares tells us it is peace: cannon and sword will be abjured, the drinking horn now symbolizes peace. Captain Cornelis Witsen holds the horn on his knee, while he shakes hands with Lieutenant Oetgens van Waveren. The civic guard was a militia responsible for maintaining law and order. In emergency they defended the city. All male citizens between 18 and 60 were supposed to serve in the guard but not everyone could because you had to buy your own arms. The twenty-five guards immortalized here could afford to have their portrait painted. They were members of the guard whose weapon was the 'voetboog' or arbalest. A narrow street in the centre of Amsterdam, the place where these guards met, still bears the name Voetboogsteeg. There are also the Handboogsteeg and the Kloveniersburgwal, named after the two other civic guards in Amsterdam, those of the long bow and of the 'klover' (a type of firearm). In each district they were divided into groups called 'vendels'. Around 1648 Amsterdam had 54 vendels.

Banquet in celebration of the Treaty of Münster
BARTHOLOMEUS VAN DER HELST
oil on canvas, 1648
232 x 547 cm

The poem by Jan Vos: Bellona [goddess of war] is sickened by blood, / Yea, Mars [god of war] curses the clash / Of menacing metal, / And the sword longs for the scabbard: / Wherefore [illegible] the valiant Wits [Witsen] / Offers the horn of Peace / To the noble Van Waveren / On the eternal treaty.

VAN DER HELST 1613-1670

The drinking horn with its depiction of St. George killing the dragon was brought out for display only on special occasions.

Another showpiece: a silver-gilt holder for a glass known as a 'bekerschroef'.

Several guards are reflected in the captain's gleaming cuirass.

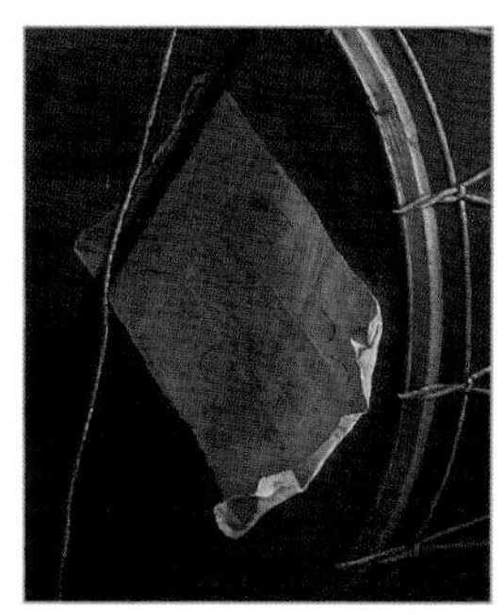

The poem on the drum.

ARTUS QUELLINUS 1609-1668

Andries de Graeff
ARTUS QUELLINUS
marble, 1661
h. 75 cm

The 50-year-old Amsterdam burgomaster Andries de Graeff had himself immortalized with his arm in a fold of his cloak, as if he were a Roman consul. The Amsterdam patricians were fond of likening themselves to their illustrious Roman predecessors. De Graeff, a scion of one of the most powerful and richest families in the city, was a burgomaster for many years. The Flemish artist Quellinus sculpted a portrait bust with a princely air. This is due not so much to De Graeff's clothes – he is in contemporary dress and wears a homely skullcap – but above all to the monumentality and the costly material. Marble, the stone in which the high and mighty traditionally had their portraits carved, is thought fitting for prominent figures in this proud bourgeois society. Through the sideward look and the slightly open mouth, Quellinus achieves the effect of a snapshot. It is as if De Graeff has been 'turned to stone' in mid-sentence.

AND.DE.GRAEFF.COS.AMST.
A.OVELLINO.F.CIƆIƆCLXI.

In translation, the inscription on the base reads: 'Andries de Graeff, Amsterdam consul, made by Quellinus in 1661'.

Ten families at most formed the upper crust of the population of Amsterdam. These 'regents' aspired to join the nobility: they bought castles and land with titles and rights, had impressive family trees drawn up and built country houses. They succeeded in extending their power by intermarrying. There were close ties, for instance, between the De Graeff and Bicker families. Andries de Graeff was married to a Bicker girl.

GERRIT ADRIAENSZ BERCKHEYDE 1638-1698

Amsterdam town hall on Dam Square
GERRIT ADRIAENSZ BERCKHEYDE
oil on canvas, 1672
33.5 x 41.5 cm

Amsterdam's new town hall was opened on 29 July 1655; the poet Constantijn Huygens called it the 'Eighth Wonder of the World'. It stands on the Dam, Amsterdam's main square, and today serves as a royal palace. This monument to civic pride was the greatest building project of the age. The first pile for the foundations was driven on 20 January 1648, shortly before peace was agreed between the Dutch Republic and Spain at Münster and the Republic became officially independent.
In a short time Amsterdam had become the centre of world trade and the most powerful city in the Republic. This power was expressed in the town hall designed by Jacob van Campen.
Gerrit Berckheyde portrays this brilliantly in this painting. Like a classical temple, the building dominates the scene. The church (the Nieuwe Kerk) next to it is dwarfed into insignificance. The front faces the Dam, the square which at that time was immediately beside the harbour. It is full of the hustle and bustle of the city. There are lots of people about: ordinary citizens, merchants and foreigners. On the right, part of the Waag, where goods were weighed, can just be seen.

The poet Constantijn Huygens called the town hall: 'the Eighth Wonder of the World, with so many Stones on high, on so much Wood beneath'. This was a reference not only to the size of the building but also to the nearly 14,000 piles which formed the foundation in the watery Amsterdam soil.

The four continents pay homage to Amsterdam
ARTUS QUELLINUS
terracotta, c. 1655
90 x 415 cm

RIGHT
The rear of the town hall, now the royal palace, where the pediment in the façade can be seen. This marble pediment is twenty metres long.

Nowhere is Amsterdam's glory as the centre of world trade in the 17th century more strikingly portrayed than in this design for the rear façade of the new town hall. This earthenware model was made in the workshop of the Flemish sculptor Quellinus. It was executed in marble, twenty metres wide, not long afterwards.

The personification of Amsterdam wearing the winged hat of Mercury, god of commerce, is enthroned in the centre. She is seated on a ship, with the globe and the gods of the Amsterdam rivers, the Amstel and the IJ, at her feet. This is how she receives the continents with their gifts. On the left is Europe, a crowned woman with a horn of plenty surrounded by bulls and cows. Beside her is Africa, half naked. She is accompanied by an elephant, a lion, snakes and two boys, one with a parrot and the other with a chameleon. The elephant's tusk, far left, recalls the trade in ivory.

To the right of Amsterdam stands Asia. She holds the reins of a camel and has a censer in her hand. Children bear Asian products: spices, tulips and jewels. Finally, the half naked woman with a feathered head dress is America. Her retinue has tobacco and sugar cane.

Amsterdam was mainly engaged in sea trade, and this is indicated by the navigation instruments at her feet.

ARTUS QUELLINUS 1609-1668

The best artists were recruited for the decoration of the town hall. The Fleming Artus Quellinus was chosen for the sculptures. He worked on them from 1650 to 1664, together with scores of assistants. He came from Antwerp but for all that time he lived in Amsterdam.

Africa wears a hat to keep off the sun. The lion and the snakes also refer to this continent.

Asia wears a turban. The tulips held by one of the children were all the rage in the Netherlands.

The reed in the crocodile's mouth refers to the cultivation of sugar cane in South America.

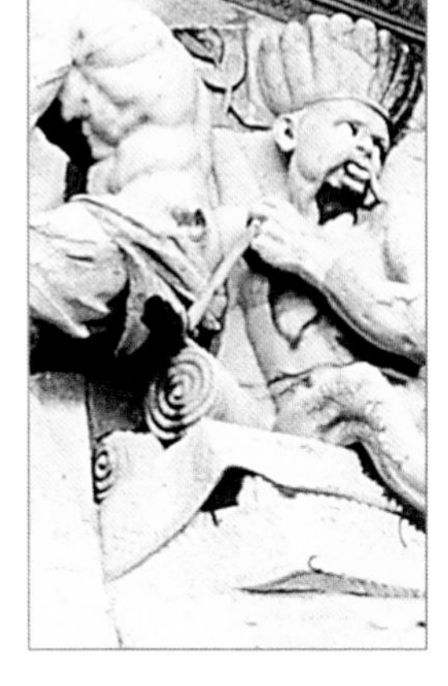

A pipe-smoking Indian next to rolls of tobacco. The miners are a reference to gold and silver from Peru.

Model ship William Rex

C. MOESMAN

wood, brass, iron, glass, rope, textile, 1698

510 x 464 x 225 cm

The strength of the Dutch Republic was its fleet. This impressive ship model was made for the Zeeland admiralty as a showpiece, a symbol of the powerful navy. Over five metres long, it is a smaller version of a large warship in every respect. It must have been made by a shipwright working for once on a smaller scale. Hull, anchors, cannons, rigging, pulleys: nothing has been forgotten. Legend has it that Admiral Cornelis Evertsen himself supervised the work.

The name William Rex – King William – refers to prince William III, who became stadholder in 1672. In 1689 he and his wife Mary Stuart also became king and queen of England. William III was very popular in Zeeland, and this is why the model was named after him.

MODEL SHIP WILLIAM REX

A warship was a fighting machine. The crew on duty operated the sails on the orders of the officers and boatswain, but carpenters were also at the ready along with sail-makers, sharpshooters, the doctor and the 'konstapel', who was in charge of munitions and cannon. The rest of the crew had to operate the guns; there were sometimes as many as eight men to a cannon. Meantime ship's boys ran back and forth bringing new cannonballs. The guns on one side of the ship were fired first. When the ship tacked, everyone ran to the other side to fire the cannon there. If all went well, finally the enemy ship was boarded. The battle then continued with hand-to-hand fighting.

The figurehead is a lion with the English crown.

In these quarter galleries were the toilets.

COUNTER DECORATION ROYAL CHARLES

Counter decoration of the English man-of-war Royal Charles

painted wood, c. 1650

277 x 378 cm

In June 1667 Admiral Michiel de Ruyter entered the Thames estuary with 80 ships and sailed up the River Medway towards Chatham, where part of the English fleet lay at anchor. At low tide a group of light Dutch ships began the attack. The chain across the river was broken, two English ships were captured, six set on fire, and the flagship *Royal Charles* was taken back to Holland in triumph. The attack came as a complete surprise. London was in panic: people fled the city and hid their valuables. 'I think the Devil shits Dutchmen,' exclaimed the Surveyor of the Navy when there was a threat of a further attack. The victory at Chatham meant the end of the Second Anglo-Dutch War (1665-1667).

The English flagship Royal Charles was scrapped. Only the counter decoration (on the stern) with the arms of the English king was preserved.

NICOLAES LOOCKEMANS †1673

Michiel de Ruyter goblet
NICOLAES LOOCKEMANS
gold and enamel, 1667
h. 30 cm, diam. 15 cm

At a banquet on 7 November 1667 Michiel de Ruyter was given this goblet by the States of Holland in gratitude for his successful attack on the English naval dockyard at Chatham. The events are depicted in enamel colours in a continuous presentation. It starts with the capture of Fort Sheerness by the Dutch, then comes Queenborough with the Dutch fleet in the background, the breaking of the chain, Chatham, Fort Upton and burning English ships. The town of Rochester is seen at the end.

Cornelis de Wit, who had sailed with the expedition as the representative of the States of Holland, received an identical goblet, as did Willem Joseph van Gendt, the deputy commander. People of high rank were often rewarded with gold or silver objects because a sum of money was felt to be inappropriate. Moreover, precious metal could always be melted down.

WILLEM VAN DE VELDE I 1611-1693

Battle of Terheide

WILLEM VAN DE VELDE I

ink on canvas, 1657

170 x 289 cm

On 9 August 1653 Admiral Maarten Harpertsz Tromp advanced with 108 ships against the English, who had 100 ships and were blockading the Dutch coast. A day later a battle took place off Terheide, south of The Hague. It was the last major battle in the First Anglo-Dutch War (1652-1654). Neither side could claim victory, but the blockade was ended. The celebrations were, however, tempered by sorrow at the death of Admiral Tromp, who had been struck by a musket ball early in the fighting.

Four years later Tromp's son Cornelis commissioned a large pen painting of the battle from Willem van de Velde. It is a detailed account of what he had seen with his own eyes.

Van de Velde depicted himself as well, with a drawing pad on his knees.

The Swede Martenson described the spectacular battle to Queen Christina. On land not only could every shot be heard, but the fighting could be clearly seen from various points on top of the dunes. From the River Maas to Petten, the beach was packed as thousands of people gathered to watch.

JOHANNES LUTMA 1584-1669

Ewer and basin

JOHANNES LUTMA

silver, 1647

ewer h. 50.4 cm

basin diam. 74.5 cm

According to family legend, this ewer and basin were owned by the 'old admiral', Maarten Harpertsz Tromp. The arms of Cornelis Tromp, Maarten's son, were added later. Cornelis was an admiral too, but unlike his famous father he was never commander-in-chief of the fleet.

Johannes Lutma made this set as a showpiece, probably for the admiralty of Amsterdam. It was given to Tromp in gratitude for his part in the capture of Dunkirk (1646), a haven for the privateers who preyed on the richly laden Dutch merchant ships.

The decoration alludes to Tromp's victory over the privateers: the sea god Neptune with a great host of creatures protects the produce of sea and land against rapacious monsters. On the basin Neptune is the focus of attention, and on the ewer Ceres, the goddess of agriculture.

Neptune.

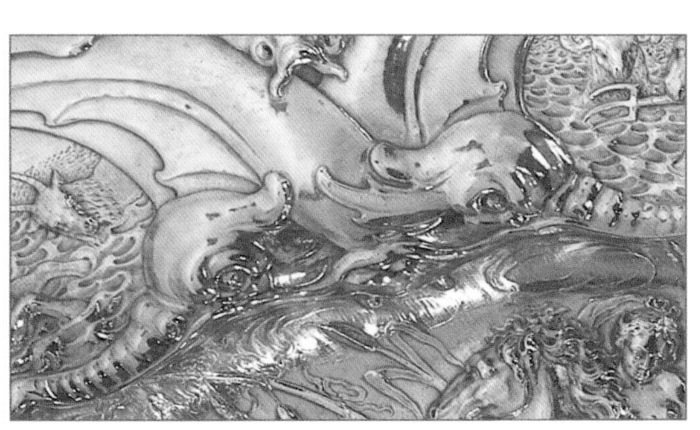

Border decoration with dolphins.

Model for the tomb of Maarten Tromp
ROMBOUT VERHULST
after a design by Jacob van Campen
terracotta and wood, c. 1654-1658
130 x 86 cm

Four days after Admiral Tromp was killed, the States General decided to commission a marble monument for his grave in the Oude Kerk in Delft as a tribute to the hugely popular hero. Bestevaer (grandfather), as the sailors called him, had a long record of service in which the great triumphs were the defeat of a Spanish armada in the Battle of the Downs (1639) and the capture of Dunkirk (1646).
The tomb was created in close collaboration between three eminent artists: Jacob van Campen and Pieter Post made the design, and Rombout Verhulst was responsible for the execution in marble. Before he began, Verhulst made this model in terracotta. The difference in colour shows that the recumbent figure was replaced by another. Eventually the model was framed and on 24 March 1654 it was presented to the States General. Shortly afterwards it was given to Tromp's family.

'Here lies the hero Tromp, gallant protector / of shipping and the sea: in the service of a free country, / that preserves his memory in artful marble / as lifelike as when he died before Holland's shore. / Mourned with cries of 'murder' and thundering cannon, / there Great Britain burning, all the water was too small a stage. / He carved himself in the hearts of the people / that image outlasts the splendour of tombstone and marble.'
(Eulogy by Joost van den Vondel (1587-1679) on the marble monument.)

Portrait of Michiel Adriaensz de Ruyter
ROMBOUT VERHULST
terracotta, 1677
h. 37 cm

ROMBOUT VERHULST 1624-1698

On 29 April 1676 Admiral Michiel de Ruyter died of the wounds he had suffered in the battle against the French off Syracuse in Sicily. This news came as a great shock. His body was embalmed and placed in a lead coffin. It was not until months later that it was shipped to the Netherlands. Michiel de Ruyter was finally buried in the Nieuwe Kerk in Amsterdam on 18 March 1677, an event which attracted large crowds. This lifelike portrait of the dead admiral is a full-size terracotta study for the head of the recumbent figure on the marble tomb made by Rombout Verhulst for the States General.

Michiel de Ruyter stirred the imagination more than the other Dutch naval heroes. He was an ordinary boy from Vlissingen who had had little education before he went to sea at the age of eleven. He showed himself to be a courageous and capable seaman, and his star rose quickly: in 1665 he was appointed lieutenant-admiral of the Dutch fleet, the highest post in the navy.

Fishing for souls

ADRIAEN PIETERSZ VAN DE VENNE

oil on panel, 1614

98.5 x 187.8 cm

On a river fishermen are busy hauling in the drowning – a miraculous catch, which is watched from the banks by hundreds of people.
The artist's contemporaries would immediately have understood the meaning of this curious scene, even without the biblical references on the front boat. The story depicted is the one in which Jesus urges his disciples to follow him: 'I will make you fishers of men'. Adriaen van de Venne gave it a form adapted to the religious and political situation of his day.
Those fishing for the souls of the drowning are Protestants and Catholics. The religious conflict was at the same time a battle for political power. The fishers' supporters on the banks leave no room for doubt about that. On the left is the Protestant Northern Netherlands with stadholder Maurice of Nassau, his brother Frederick Henry and their allies behind a branch of an orange tree. On the right is the Catholic South with the archduke Albert and his wife Isabella, the Spanish commander Spinola and the Pope borne by cardinals.
It is clear where the artist's sympathies lie: on the Protestant side the trees have leaves, while on the other side they are withering.

ADRIAEN

The fishers' attributes indicate to which faith they belong.
The Protestants, on the left, fish with the aid of the Bible and faith, hope and love, as is written on the nets. The Catholics, led by a bishop, fish with hymns and church vessels fore and aft in the boat.

Archduke Albert and his wife Isabella.

In the forefront of the Protestant camp stands the painter himself, with his hand at his waist.

PIETERSZ VAN DE VENNE 1589-1652

Protestant souls are fished up.

Originally the Catholic nets were empty. The people were added later.

The family of Orange and their allies.

The big bluebottle is a joke by the painter. It looks just like a real fly.

MICHIEL JANSZ VAN MIEREVELT 1567-1641

Portrait of Maurits, Prince of Orange
MICHIEL JANSZ VAN MIEREVELT
oil on panel, c. 1613-1620
220.3 x 143.5 cm

Maurits is portrayed here as the commander of the army, with a baton in his hand. He is wearing the ceremonial suit of gilt armour given to him by the States General after his victory at Nieuwpoort (1600).
Maurits was a brilliant general who succeeded in rapidly reforming the army to make it a modern fighting force. Under his command a great deal of territory was captured from the Spanish. When the truce with Spain came into effect in 1609, the whole country north of the great rivers as well as the province of Zeeland had been liberated.
In 1613 Maurits was made a Knight of the Order of the Garter by James I of England. This was an important sign of international recognition for the stadholder of the young Republic. Shortly afterwards the States General commissioned a state portrait of Maurits with the insignia of the Order at his neck.

ADRIAEN PIETERSZ VAN DE VENNE 1589-1652

Princes Maurits and Frederik Hendrik at the Valkenburg horse fair, 1618

ADRIAEN PIETERSZ VAN DE VENNE

oil on panel, 1618

55.5 x 134.5 cm

The popular horse fair and 'kermis' in the village of Valkenburg near Leiden was an annual event. Stadholder Maurits and his brother Frederik Hendrik are seen arriving at the fair in 1618 with considerable pomp and ceremony.

Maurits coach is drawn by six greys, a privilege reserved for rulers. At the beginning of 1618 Maurits had become Prince of Orange, a hereditary title that he acquired on the death of his half brother.

Maurits status at the courts of Europe, as the representative of the small seafaring nation that dominated world trade, was further increased by his princely title. This was also true in his home country.

The prince's arrival is watched by an awestruck crowd of peasants, townspeople and stall holders. Some of them raise their hats respectfully.

Johan de Hertoghe, prince Maurits favourite courtier, and his wife.

Fairground attraction with dressed monkeys.

The vegetable-seller does not notice that she is being robbed.

Six princely greys.

JOHAN VAN OLDENBARNEVELT

Execution sword

iron, c. 1600-1625

110 x 22.6 cm

Johan van Oldenbarnevelt's walking-stick

wood, iron, ivory, c. 1600-1625

96 cm

On 13 May 1619, with his upper body bare and leaning heavily on his cane, the aged Van Oldenbarnevelt appeared on the scaffold in front of the Ridderzaal of the Binnenhof in The Hague. There the statesman was beheaded with a sword. 'Make it short, make it short' were his last words, after he had once more emphatically stated that he had always acted sincerely and devoutly, like a good patriot.
The cane and the sword took on an almost religious significance for Van Oldenbarnevelt's followers. Long after his death they were cherished like relics. But there is absolutely no proof of their authenticity. The same claim is made for no less than three canes. The one that is kept together with the manuscript of Joost van den Vondel's poem 'To the cane' (c. 1657) in the Amsterdam University Library is probably the true one.

A poem was engraved on the blade of the sword in the 18th century: 'Aged, blameless hero, / Ill-fated Oldenbarnevelt / This sword struck through your neck / A deep wound in the State's advisor / When on the scaffold in The Hague / Your precious life was cut short.'

HUGO GROTIUS

This may be the chest in which Grotius escaped from Loevestein Castle in 1621, where he had been imprisoned since 1619. The scholar spent his days there studying and writing. A bookseller arranged for new books to be sent to him regularly and for the old ones to be collected. This gave Grotius's wife the brilliant idea of having her husband escape in the chest used to transport the books. The trick worked and via Gorinchem and Antwerp Grotius fled to Paris, where he was joined later by his wife and children. Grotius lived there in exile until his death, and wrote his best-known works there. This daring feat caused a stir at home and abroad. 'One woman is more formidable than a thousand men,' wrote Joost van den Vondel later.

Hugo Grotius' bookchest

pine, leather, iron, c. 1600-1615

72 x 159 x 75 cm

NASSAU TUNIC

Nassau tunic

silk, linen, metal thread, 1647

86 x 125 cm

This garment was made for the funeral of stadholder Frederick Henry on 10 May 1647 in Delft. It is embroidered with the arms of the House of Orange Nassau, as borne by Frederick Henry. They are made up of several arms indicating the prince's noble titles. This kind of tunic had a symbolic function. It was carried on a pole in the funeral procession.

Frederick Henry was an outstanding strategist. He was known as 'the city slayer' because he had captured a series of cities from the Spanish. Together with his wife Amalia van Solms, he considerably increased the status and wealth of the House of Orange Nassau. They maintained a regal household, built magnificent palaces and managed to arrange an extraordinarily good marriage for their son with Mary Stuart, princess of England.

DIRCK VAN DELEN 1605-1671

Assembly of the States General
DIRCK VAN DELEN
oil on panel and metal
c. 1651-1671
52 x 66 cm

The assembly is painted on a hinged copper plate that can be lifted up. The other side shows a partition with a series of tapestries.

The sudden death of the 24-year-old stadholder William II in October 1650 was the reason for convening a meeting of the over 300 representatives of the seven provinces, the States General. From 18 January to 21 August 1651 they discussed the constitutional future of the Republic. The delegates from the powerful province of Holland, as always primarily interested in trade and peace, did not want another stadholder after the experience of armed conflicts with the hot-headed William II, and they also wanted to curb the power of the army. They got their way. The States themselves now held power. They managed to bring about the ideal of 'true liberty' for which Oldenbarnevelt had died and Grotius had gone into exile. The Great Assembly was held in the Great Hall of the Binnenhof in The Hague, now called the Ridderzaal, which was specially decorated for the occasion. The banners are trophies captured from the Spanish and Portuguese.

JAN STEEN 1626-1679

Prince's Day
JAN STEEN
oil on panel
c. 1660-1670
46 x 62.5 cm

It is Prince's Day, 14 November, the birthday of William III. The young Prince of Orange was well-liked, especially by the 'common people'. His birthday is reason enough for a party at the inn. When this work was painted, the political situation in the Netherlands was not stable. There was no stadholder and some people, the supporters of the States General, were quite happy with that. But those who favoured the Prince wanted a stadholder again. To them little William was a living symbol. There are partisans of both sides at the inn, for not everyone joins in the toast.

The Prince's portrait hangs on the wall, hats sport orange ribbons and feathers, and in the foreground is an orange, a familiar symbol of the House of Orange Nassau. The landlord proposes a toast. 'To the health of the Nassau line / In one hand a rapier (sword), in the other the glass,' says the piece of paper.

Hat with orange ribbon.

Note with inscription.

Portrait of the prince.

Bell frame with the motto of opponents of the House of Orange.

ATTRIBUTED TO JAN DE BAEN 1633-1702

The bodies of the De Witt brothers
ATTRIBUTED TO
JAN DE BAEN
oil on canvas, c. 1672-1675
69.5 x 56 cm

In the 'Year of Disaster', 1672, the Republic was at its lowest point. The country was under attack on all sides. The strength of the army had been seriously undermined by years of economizing, and panic swept the country. There were loud calls for a strong leader. The province of Zeeland took the initiative and appointed the 22-year-old William III stadholder and commander-in-chief of the army and navy. The other provinces followed suit. At this, grand pensionary Johan de Witt, the highest government official, resigned. A scapegoat had to be found and the Orange supporters pointed at Johan and Cornelis de Witt. An enraged mob attacked the two brothers on 20 August. It was premeditated murder: the mob was given the chance to lynch them and to drag the corpses to the scaffold. The dead leaders were hung from the gallows for all to see. Severed limbs were offered for sale and the people sang: 'Up with Orange, down with De Witts. / Let lightning strike all who differ.'

Amsterdam as the centre of world trade
PIETER ISAACSZ
oil on panel, c. 1606-1607
79.4 x 165 cm

In 1604, two years after the Dutch East India Company was founded, Jan Pietersz Sweelinck, the city organist of Amsterdam, travelled to Antwerp to order a new harpsichord for the city from the renowned Ruckers family of instrument makers. Amsterdam had great faith in the Company: the world lay at the city's feet. Peter Isaacsz expressed this far-sighted view on the lid of the harpsichord. The design was by Karel van Mander.

PIETER ISAACSZ 1569-1625

The personification of Amsterdam is enthroned on the left, between female figures with a ship and a string of pearls, the symbols of seafaring and riches. In her right hand she is holding a horn of plenty, while her other hand rests on a celestial globe. Two seamen consult the globe. At her feet the river gods recline and beside her stands the sea god Neptune with his trident. And just behind him is the painter himself.

In the centre are three East Indiamen. The biggest is probably the flagship Mauritius, named after the stadholder Maurice of Nassau. His arms are on the stern. Behind them the whole world is pictured, as seen from the North Pole with Europe in the foreground and Africa beyond. The island Madagascar, on the left, is clearly recognisable. On the far left lies the Indonesian archipelago and on the far right America. At the lower right, lastly, there is an oriental scene with a mosque and a Hindu temple.

DANIËL VERTANGEN c. 1600 - c. 1684

Portraits of Jan Valckenburgh and Dina Lems

DANIËL VERTANGEN

oil on canvas, c. 1660

128.3 x 102 cm

Jan Valckenburgh, Director-General of the Gold Coast, poses proudly in about 1660. In the background is Fort Elmina, the principal stronghold on the Gold Coast, which the West India Company had captured from the Portuguese in 1637.
Beside the Director-General stands a negro boy displaying Valckenburgh's gold medal – an indirect reference to the lucrative trade in gold and slaves conducted through this outpost. At first the gold trade was the more important; dealing in slaves developed in the course of the 17th century. They were bought from African dealers, then shipped to South America and there sold to plantation owners.
The portrait of Valckenburgh's wife also has an African background. Next to her is a coffee plant.

Fort Elmina was built by the Portuguese in 1482 to protect the trade in the gold mined in the interior. They named it Sao Jorge del Mina, Elmina – the mine – for short. Elmina stayed in Dutch hands until 1872, when it was sold to the British.

HENDRIK VAN SCHUYLENBURG c. 1620-1689

VOC base at Hougly in Bengal

HENDRIK VAN SCHUYLENBURG

oil on canvas, 1665

203 x 316 cm

This scene is set in India. The VOC post at Hougly (Bengal) on the Ganges was the finest in all Asia. One visitor in 1664 thought it looked more like a 'splendid castle' than an office. The Dutch flag is prominent and Dutch ships are on the river.

Life in and around the factory or trading agency is depicted as in a strip cartoon: carrying goods under Dutch supervision, strolling in the garden and bathing the horses. Local rituals are also shown: the cremation of a body by the river and a torture scene in the background on the right. In front of them is the encampment of a Bengali dignitary who presides in the big tent. A procession of high VOC officials is heading towards him with the annual gifts. It was important to keep up trading contacts. Bengal was the Company's most profitable post, the main commodities traded being cotton and saltpetre.

Indian prince.

Dutch dignitary.

Cremation of a body.

Elephant.

KENDI

This Chinese porcelain elephant is a jug for water, known as a 'kendi' in Malay; the two tusks are the spouts. It is decorated with chrysanthemums and swastikas, Chinese symbols of geniality and longevity respectively.

The kendi was recovered in 1976 from the wreck of the Witte Leeuw, an East Indiaman lost with all hands in 1613 off the island of St. Helena in the Atlantic while on its voyage home. She had engaged two Portuguese ships when, at the height of the battle, a cannon exploded, and she blew up and sank. The loss of the ship and her cargo cost the VOC millions, for in addition to porcelain she had on board large quantities of nutmeg and pepper.

Kendi

porcelain, early 17th century

h. 17 cm

What the Witte Leeuw was carrying is known from the cargo lists. Apart from hundreds of pieces of porcelain, there were 125 sacks of nutmeg (c. 900 kg), 15,171 sacks of pepper (c. 100,000 kg) and 1317 diamonds. The total value was estimated at 8.5 million guilders.

CRADLE

This ebony cradle was made in Asia and, like other oriental furniture, was not meant for export. It would have been made to order for a VOC official for his own use or as a gift for a prince. It probably comes from the Coromandel Coast of India, where this type of wood is found. The decoration and carving as well as the use of ivory also point in this direction.

The cradle is a superb mix of West and East. It has the usual European form, and the decoration with small balusters is also Western. But the carving at the head and foot is in part Eastern: a tangle of curls, shoots and mythical creatures such as the mermaids with expressive heads. Hindu motifs include the elephant head of the god Ganesa and the fish-like sea creatures, the makaras.

Black-brown ebony was imported to the Netherlands early in the 17th century and was used in furniture-making.

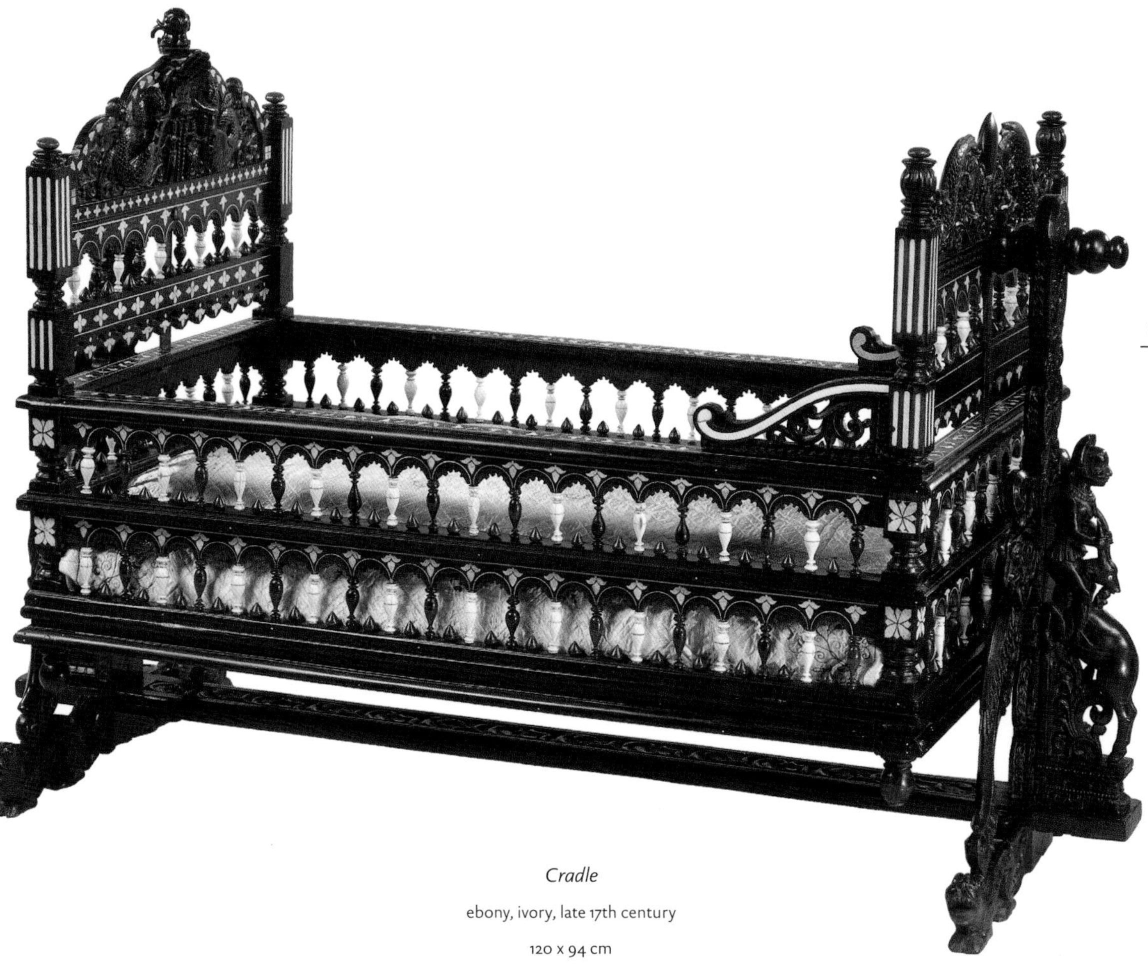

Cradle

ebony, ivory, late 17th century

120 x 94 cm

At the head of the cradle is Ganesa. This Hindu deity is the god of the beginning. A child stands at the beginning of life. So Ganesa's blessing is essential, especially for a Dutch child in foreign parts.

JACOB JANSZ COEMAN †1672

Jacob Coeman painted this portrait of Pieter Cnoll and his family at Batavia, the VOC's headquarters in Asia. The prosperity of the family is evident: fashionably dressed, they pose against a villa-like background, together with two of their fifty slaves. Oentoeng, the family's pajong or parasol carrier, here holds the banner of the civic guard of which Cnoll was a member. Daughter Cornelia has an ivory jewel box on her lap, the kind of luxury object adored by Europeans in Batavia.

Cnoll had been in Batavia since 1647, where he had risen to the high rank of first senior merchant, in charge of the bookkeeping for all Asia. In 1652 he married Cornelia van Nieuwenrode, the daughter of a VOC official in Hirado in Japan and a Japanese courtesan. After their father died, Cornelia and her sister were taken from their mother and put in the orphanage at Batavia.

The Cnoll family
JACOB JANSZ COEMAN
oil on canvas, 1665
130 x 190.5 cm

Jewel case.

FRANS POST c. 1612-1680

View of Olinda, Brazil

FRANS POST

oil on canvas, 1662

107.5 x 172.5 cm

Frans Post painted this Brazilian landscape eighteen years after his return to the Netherlands. It is a nostalgic fantasy in which the flora and fauna receive most attention. Post used drawings he had made on the spot, but had evidently forgotten the correct dimensions, for the proportions are all wrong. Frans Post and his colleague Albert Eckhout were the first European painters to depict Brazil. They were there from 1637 to 1644 with a military expedition led by John Maurice, Count of Nassau-Siegen. The West India Company appointed him governor of the territory captured from the Portuguese in Pernambuco. He saw to it that the expedition included scientists and artists as well as troops and merchants.

John Maurice arrived in the Netherlands in 1644 with a large collection of 'Braziliana': weapons, everyday objects, dried plants, stuffed animals, drawings, paintings and even a few Indians. Much of the collection was later given away by John Maurice or sold, and in 1679 Louis XIV of France acquired several dozen of Post's landscapes.

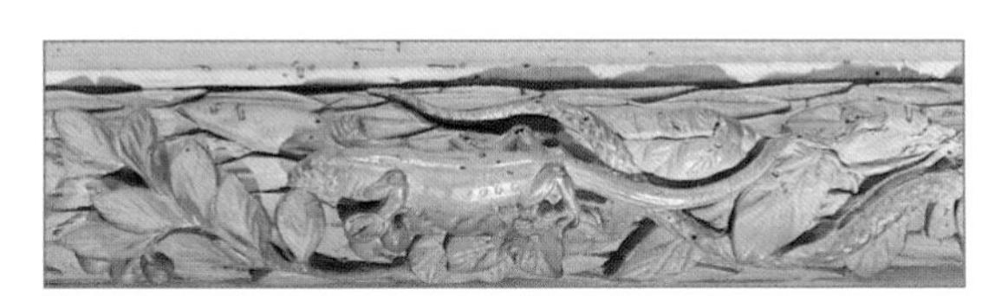

The frame was probably ordered at the same time as the painting. The same animals and plants are seen in the painting and in the carving.

THE INTERIOR

THE DUTCH DOLLS HOUSE

The prosperity of the Dutch in the Golden Age was reflected in the houses they owned. Just how expensively they were furnished is shown by two dolls houses from Amsterdam which were assembled by wealthy women, not as toys but as a hobby. They are family homes in miniature that present a complete picture of life in a fashionable Amsterdam household in the Golden Age. Painters also recorded the Dutch interior. They reveal other aspects of daily life, among not only the rich but also the less fortunate.

• pages 44-53

PRINCELY SILVER

The Republic's affluence is also apparent from the many silver objects made in the Golden Age. Some of the hundreds of silversmiths who made their living from this trade were outstandingly gifted. They did not make objects for everyday use but rather works of art that were admired and collected as such. Foremost among them were the Utrecht brothers Adam and Paulus van Vianen. The younger of them, Paulus (c. 1570-1613), was the most highly valued artist at the court of the Emperor Rudolf II in Prague. Adam (1568/69-1627), who spent his entire life in Utrecht, was equally successful. His patrons were connoisseurs and collectors in the Republic.

• pages 54-59

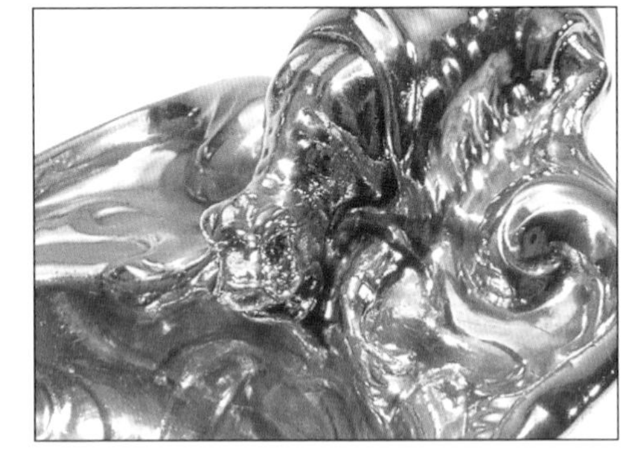

THE SPLENDOUR OF AMSTERDAM

Johannes Lutma (1587-1669) was the leading figure in the next generation of silversmiths. He was one of the many artists who came from far and wide to try their luck in thriving Amsterdam. Contemporaries greatly admired Lutma. He was unrivalled in his ability to shape silver to suit the opulent taste of the Amsterdam merchants.

• pages 60-61

PRINCELY BRONZE

The sculptor Adriaen de Vries (1556-1626) was born in The Hague but moved abroad early in his career. And like Paulus van Vianen he eventually ended up in Prague. In 1602 he became the widely acclaimed court sculptor of Rudolf II. After the emperor's death in 1612, De Vries stayed on in Prague, where eminent patrons still came to him.

• pages 62-63

WILLIAM AND MARY

The decorative arts in the later part of the Golden Age bore the stamp of Prince William III and the English Princess Mary Stuart, whom he married in 1677. They built and furnished palaces and laid out beautiful gardens. Especially after they were crowned king and queen of England in 1689, there was a huge upsurge of building activity. For those working in the decorative arts this was a golden opportunity to display their skills.

• pages 64-69

DELFTWARE

Delft earthenware decorated in blue underwent great changes. This ware, which was proudly known as 'Hollants porceleyn' because of its outward similarity to Chinese porcelain, was already extraordinarily popular by around 1660. Millions of pieces were made for use at table or to decorate a mantelpiece or cabinet. Plates, vases, jugs, plaques, inkpots, shoes and a host of other objects found their way into people's homes. They were thought to be fascinating objects not only in the Republic but far beyond.

• pages 64-69

PRINCELY FURNITURE

Furniture in the late 17th century mirrored the taste of the court of Louis XIV in France. All European rulers followed the French lead, and so did William and Mary. After they were crowned in 1689, furniture of princely status was much in demand with both the royal couple themselves and the circles around them. They followed the dictates of fashion at the French court, despite the fact that Louis XIV was William's political opponent.

• pages 70-73

Petronella's dolls house was famous. Visitors from the Netherlands and abroad came to see it, among them Zacharias von Uffenbach from Germany, who in 1718 was given a demonstration lasting three hours. A doll was picked up and her 'Dutch' underwear studied, the contents of cupboards were examined and books from the library were admired. The pump in the kitchen was demonstrated, but the fountain in the garden was found not to be in working order.

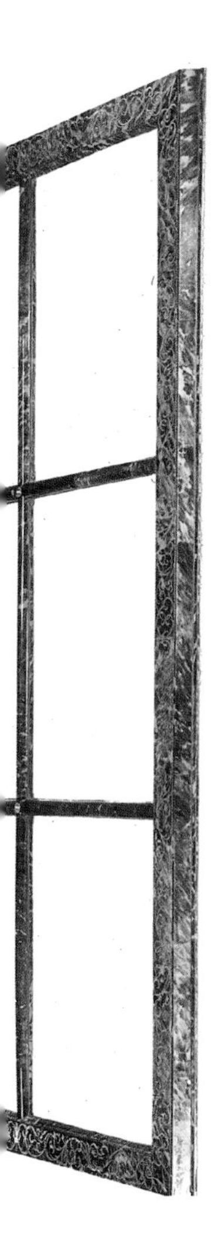

The dolls house of

PETRONELLA OORTMAN

Amsterdam, c. 1686-1710

oak, veneered with tortoiseshell and inlaid with pewter

225 x 189.5 x 78 cm

DOLLS HOUSE OORTMAN

The dolls house owned by Petronella Oortman, the wealthy wife of a merchant, was seen early on as one of the wonders of the world. It is fully furnished, and each item is made exactly to size, always on a scale of 1:9. As far as possible each object was made of the same material that would have been used for a full-size object.

A large number of craftsmen were involved: painters, carvers, furniture-makers, basket weavers, silversmiths, glassblowers, bookbinders. They made the approximately 700 objects in the house, household items of which full-size examples have rarely been preserved. The dolls house gives a unique picture of the interior of a wealthy family's home and how the household was run in the late 17th century.

Just to furnish her dolls house, Petronella Oortman paid an amount that would easily have been enough to buy an expensive canal house. The exterior, veneered with tortoiseshell and inlaid with pewter, was also very costly.

The house has three floors. The middle one is the most important and has the most expensively furnished rooms, clearly intended for receiving guests. The attic floor is the domain of the servants. Here are the linen room and the peat loft, where goods are stored and the maids sleep in small rooms. The nursery is here too. In the basement are the kitchens, one for use and one for display. A tapestry room and a library are also found here.

The back of Petronella Oortman's dolls house.

In the linen room the washing was dealt with after it came back from the laundry. There are rods for hanging up clothes to dry, a linen press, an ironing table with irons, laundry baskets and a clothes tray. At the back are the maids' sleeping quarters, each with a box bed, a chair and a chamber pot.

The irons are made of brass with an iron sole-plate and a wooden handle. Glowing charcoal was put inside them. When not in use, the iron rested on a stand.

The nursery is furnished entirely in yellow silk trimmed with a blue band. The use of the same fabric throughout is characteristic of the late 17th century. The bed is a 'pavilion bed', so called because of the canopy hanging from the ceiling. The cabinet contains children's clothes.

This is the most expensively furnished room, the salon, which was used only for receptions. It is decorated all round with wall paintings of a landscape, and on the ceiling is a cloudy sky. As was the custom, the chairs are lined up along the walls. But in the middle two are placed ready for a game of backgammon.
The porcelain pots are cuspidors for spitting out tobacco juice.

The chairs are more elaborate than those in other rooms.

As the name implies, the best kitchen was where the finest kitchenware was put on show. It was used for eating but not for cooking. The whole back wall is taken up by a well-filled porcelain cabinet. The porcelain comes from China and Japan. The cupboards below contain glassware. There is also a child's commode and on the table a sewing pillow.

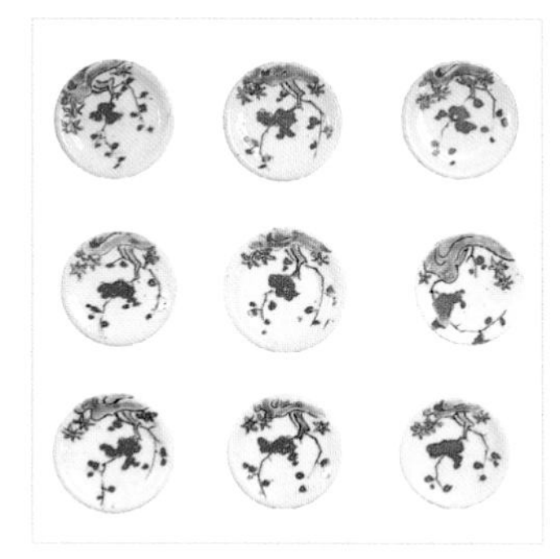

Most of the porcelain was bought from the Dutch East India Company, which traded in doll's items from an early staage. These dishes from Arita in Japan were probably made to order.

DOLLS HOUSE DUNOIS

The dolls house of

PETRONELLA DUNOIS

Amsterdam, c. 1676

oak, veneered with walnut

200 x 149 x 56 cm

A tiny pin cushion bears the date 1676. Yet not everything in Petronella Dunois's dolls house is 17th century. Over time things have continued to be added to the house. As a result, the rooms are rather full and less harmoniously furnished than those in Petronella Oortman's house. Moreover, the proportions are not always right, but that has its own charm. For example, the silver linen press in the linen room is very small, while the brushes are quite large. It is likely that Petronella had already bought these objects before she had the house.

What makes this dolls house so special is not only the 212 silver miniatures placed here and there, but above all the liveliness of the interiors. This is because of the wax dolls. There are twenty of them and they show great variety: distinguished residents, ordinary servants, children and visitors. They are all dressed for the role allocated to them. In the lying-in room, for example, the mother, who has given birth to twins, lies in bed. The dry-nurse, wearing an apron, stands beside her, while the wet-nurse, in traditional costume, has a swaddled baby on a christening cloth on her lap. The other child lies naked in the cradle. The distinguished gentleman, finally, is the father.

When there was a baby on the way, a lying-in room was organized. Visitors could also be received there, so the room is attractively furnished. The chintz hangings from India on the walls and the bed were a novelty in 1676. The screen is Japanese.

Child in a walking frame in the nursery. This room is lively not only because of the three children and their baby-sitter but also because of the toys lying here and there.

The new mother in bed.

The well-stocked linen chest in the salon or best room.

PIETER DE HOOCH 1629-1684

Interior with women beside a linen chest
PIETER DE HOOCH
oil on canvas, 1663
70 x 75.5 cm

A glimpse inside the house of a well-to-do family. Two women are putting away the crisply ironed linen. The lady of the house puts it in the chest herself, while her daughter holds up the pile. Meanwhile the son plays with his 'kolf' stick and ball.
A well-filled linen chest was the pride and joy of every housewife and the showpiece in the house. That certainly goes for this oak chest inlaid with ebony.
Through the opening the entrance hall can just be seen, and beyond it the canal and a house opposite. Such through views are typical of Pieter de Hooch, the master of the Dutch interior.

Laundry basket and clothes tray.

The wealthy generally sent their linen out for washing, about twice a year or more often. It came back damp and folded, after which it was dried, ironed, beaten, mangled, folded and pressed in the linen room. This was a time-consuming job for which extra staff were often hired.

GERARD TER BORCH 1617-1681

Galant conversation, known as 'The paternal admonition'
GERARD TER BORCH
oil on canvas, c. 1654
71 x 73 cm

A four-poster was the most expensive piece of furniture in the house in the 17th century. Accordingly, it was often placed in the 'best room', which was used for receptions. The room in this painting by Gerard ter Borch is, however, rather sparsely furnished, for apart from the bed there is only a table and some chairs. It is only a small company. The centre of attention is the elegant woman in the gleaming satin dress. She is being addressed by a young man, but how she reacts is hidden from the viewer. Meanwhile the other woman quietly sips her wine.
What is portrayed here with such refinement looks like a pleasant tête-à-tête, but on closer consideration it appears more like a business conversation between a prostitute, a client and a procuress.

The toilet glass and the powder brush in combination with the bed indicate that this is a brothel scene.

As early as the 18th century the ambiguity of this scene was no longer understood. The work, then called 'The paternal admonition', must have been quite popular. In his Wahlverwandtschaften Goethe tells of a company which presented the scene as a 'tableau vivant'.

WILLEM BUYTEWECH 1591/92-1624

Dignified couples courting
WILLEM BUYTEWECH
oil on canvas, c. 1616-1620
56.3 x 70.5 cm

As the title suggests, this painting is about love. The couple on the right have found one another, but with the two on the left the courtship is not yet settled. The woman plays a game with the man beside her. She is holding two roses and he is allowed to choose one without looking. With it he chooses one of the ladies. What he does not see is that the woman has already decided on her choice: her hands are crossed, so right becomes left and left right. The woman has the man caught in her web. The spider's web on the window bars, behind the coat of arms, may be symbolic, like the wall fountain that here stands for the source of love.

The young people are dressed in the very height of fashion. Willem Buytewech had an eye for that kind of thing. Around 1615 he portrayed the various fashions prevailing among the wealthy young people of Europe in a series of etchings. These prints were very popular.

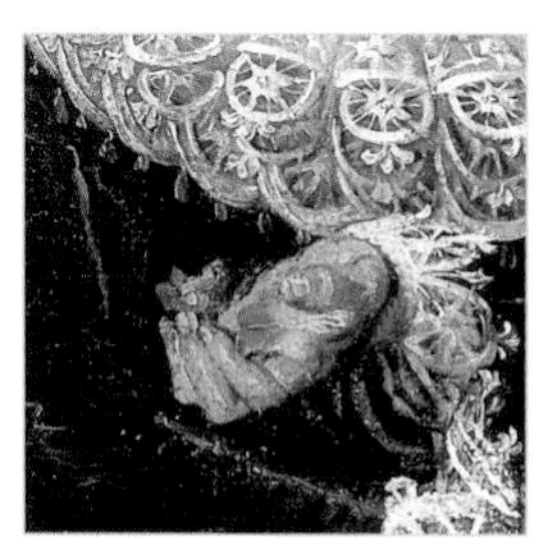

QUIRINGH VAN BREKELENKAM c. 1620-1668

The tailor's workshop
QUIRINGH VAN BREKELENKAM
Oil on canvas, 1661
66 x 53 cm

The room on the street side might be furnished as living quarters, but often it was a shop or a workshop, as here. The painting shows a tailor and his apprentices in his workshop sitting on the table in front of the window. This gives them a good light by which to work. While the boys keep on working away, the tailor pauses to speak to a client. She has just brought the jacket on the table. On her arm she has a bucket for her shopping.
Quiringh van Brekelenkam depicted numerous craftsmen. The tailor was a favourite. This was one of the luxury trades in the wealthy Dutch cities and was held in high regard in the 17th century. This is evident from this workshop. There is even a rather nice landscape on the wall.

Iron on the tiles.

Scissors and pin on the table.

Stories about the gods and goddesses of classical antiquity were popular in the 17th century. Paulus van Vianen made this sublime masterpiece shortly before his death: a ewer and basin with mythological scenes in which Diana, the goddess of the hunt, has the leading role.

The basin shows the fate of Actaeon, the hunter who spied on Diana while she was bathing. When the goddess spotted him, she transformed him into a deer. This was a severe punishment, for Actaeon was to be killed by his own dogs.

Van Vianen shows this scene on the back of the basin, which was meant to be a spectacular work of art, rather than actually used. The back could be shown as a surprise.

The ewer shows the story of Diana's companion Callisto, who was seduced by Jupiter disguised as Diana. This is the scene on the front. What happened to her subsequently is depicted on the other side. Callisto proved to be pregnant, whereupon Diana struck her and turned her into a bear. When she was almost killed by her own son, Jupiter intervened. He placed mother and son in the heavens as stars (the Great Bear and the Little Bear).

Basin and ewer with Diana and Actaeon, and Diana and Callisto
PAULUS VAN VIANEN
silver, 1613
basin diam. 52.3 cm
ewer h. 34 cm

PAULUS VAN VIANEN c. 1570-1613

Diana splashes water at the hunter. Antlers are growing from his hat.

The signature 'PV' and the date.

The border is decorated with a new kind of ornament. Folds of skin, flabby flesh, bones, tendons, heads of monsters and molluscs appear to have been the inspiration for the curious auricular style. 'Whimsy and drollery' was how these fantastical ornaments were known in the 17th century; the Dutch term 'kwabornament' dates from the 19th century. Paulus van Vianen played a large part in the development of this style. It became popular and left its mark on Dutch decorative art for much of the 17th century.

The Adoration of the shepherds

PAULUS VAN VIANEN

silver, 1607

31.8 x 22.9 cm

PAULUS VAN VIANEN

In 1605 and 1607 Paulus van Vianen made two silver reliefs with Christ in the leading role: the adoration of the shepherds at his birth and his resurrection from death. They are virtuoso works in which with extremely fine relief he achieved an effect comparable with the atmospheric effects produced by painters in oils. How Paulus van Vianen was able to turn flat, thin plates of silver into such detailed depictions is almost incomprehensible. He did it by chasing the scene into the silver with punches and hammers. The reliefs are sometimes very low, then high. On a few occasions he used a different technique. The two shepherds in the foreground of the 'Adoration', for example, were cast and attached to the plaque later.

Van Vianen made many drawings in the surroundings of Prague. He used them for his reliefs, and this is why his figures and landscapes look so realistic. Emperor Rudolf II must have been a great admirer of Van Vianen's artistry and craftsmanship. He probably kept masterpieces like these in a collector's cabinet so that he could study them often.

The Resurrection of Christ

PAULUS VAN VIANEN

silver, 1605

31 x 22 cm

Signature 'PV' and date.

The women are on their way to the grave.

Basin and ewer

ADAM VAN VIANEN

gilt silver, 1614

basin diam. 52.5 cm

ewer h. 38.5 cm

ADAM VAN

The notable feature of this ewer and basin is the decoration with martial scenes. They are all Dutch victories over the Spanish from the first half of the Eighty Year War. Most of them occurred under Prince Maurice. His greatest triumph, the Battle of Nieuwpoort in 1600, is depicted in the centre of the basin.

Adam van Vianen probably made this ewer and basin for the city of Amsterdam. The fact that the city gave the commission to a silversmith from Utrecht tells us something about Adam's reputation and skill. The set was intended as a tribute to Maurice and was probably used when he attended a banquet in Amsterdam. The city had close ties with Maurice at that time. He would have been the only person allowed to wash his hands above the basin, while a servant poured water from the ewer.

VIANEN c. 1569-1627

Ewer

ADAM VAN VIANEN

gilt silver, 1614

h. 25.5 cm

This ewer consists entirely of auricular ornament; it is a mass of movement, with one form dissolving into the next. The result is an almost abstract sculpture in which figures can be discerned here and there. The foot is a squatting monkey, the handle a long-haired woman bending forwards and ending in the nostrils of a monster. From the cover rises a sea monster and when the cover is lifted two lizards can be seen.

Adam van Vianen made this ewer and the basin and ewer on page 58 in the same year. The commission again came from Amsterdam, but this time from the guild of silversmiths. They wanted to pay tribute to their celebrated colleague Paulus van Vianen, who died in Prague in 1613. Adam was widely acclaimed for this work of art, which was chased from virtually a single piece of silver. Painters depicted the ewer scores of times.

Two salt-cellars

JOHANNES LUTMA

silver, partly gilded, 1639

24.2 x 12 cm

Salt-cellars were the showpieces on the table. This set is an excellent example. The salt trays, in the form of large shells, are borne on the heads of plump boys on dolphins. They hold a shell and a piece of coral, and at their feet are more shells. The theme of the sea – from which salt is obtained – even extends to the base. Fish heads are incorporated into the auricular ornament. These salt-cellars were already famous in the 17th century.

The salt trade was a thriving business in the Golden Age. Apart from at table, salt was used in industry and in fishing, where the herring fishers were the biggest customers. Salt was not extracted in the Netherlands, as it is now, but imported from the Mediterranean area and countries in Central America. That made it expensive.

JOHANNES LUTMA 1584-1669

This dish was chased from a single piece of silver. It consists entirely of slithery auricular ornaments dissolving into each other. At the bottom wide-open jaws can be seen, but at the sides it looks like a human skull. The handle is even more extraordinary: a tortoise-like creature sticks its head down as if about to drink from the dish.

Dish

JOHANNES LUTMA

silver, 1641

7.8 x 20.3 x 15 cm

As a true artist, Lutma signed this piece underneath. The unusual signature is not the only indication that he was proud of it. In Rembrandt's etched portrait of his friend Lutma it stands on the table beside him.

Bacchus discovers Ariadne on Naxos

ADRIAEN DE VRIES

bronze, c. 1610-1612

52.5 x 42 cm

The man abruptly pulls the curtain aside and sees a girl fast asleep. A satyr with hairy goat's legs holds up a torch to give him light. This mythical creature makes it clear that what is depicted here is not just any bedroom scene. It is an episode from a mythological tale, the love story of Bacchus and Ariadne.
Adriaen de Vries portrayed it in bronze in a masterly fashion. He deviated from the original story, in which Ariadne was found on the beach, and turned it into an erotically charged scene with naked figures. It is a dramatic moment, almost like a snapshot.

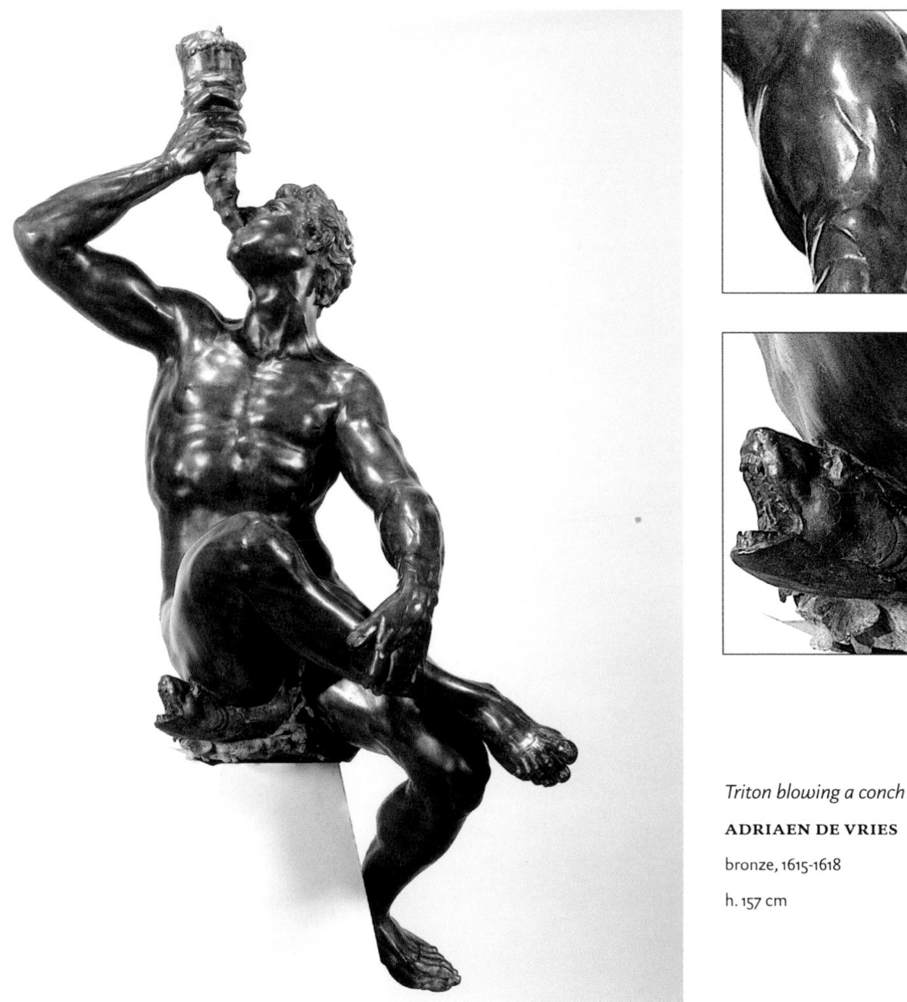

Triton blowing a conch

ADRIAEN DE VRIES

bronze, 1615-1618

h. 157 cm

ADRIAEN DE VRIES c. 1556-1626

Even more dramatic is this triton, a mythical sea creature from the retinue of Neptune, god of the sea. By blowing on his conch, he can whip up the waves or calm them down. The triton is sculpted with great realism: the veins and muscles are so convincing that the figure seems to come to life.
A close look reveals that the triton was part of a fountain: water used to spout from the shell and the fish's mouth. Together with two other tritons, he belonged to the monumental Neptune fountain made by Adriaen de Vries between 1615 and 1618 for the Danish king Christian IV for his new castle, Frederiksborg.

De Vries made the sculptures in Prague. When they were finished they were transported to Denmark, where the fountain was assembled in the forecourt of Frederiksborg Castle. In 1659 the work was dismantled by Swedish troops and taken to Sweden as war booty.

Plate

faience, 1658

diam. 20.5 cm

This plate with the portrait of the young Prince William III of Orange has the form of a breakfast plate. Yet it would never have been used for that purpose. It would have had a prominent place in the home of an admirer of the prince. Plates like this were popular for a long time among his supporters. The oranges in the border allude to the House of Orange.

DELFTWARE

Delftware (faience) was developed in an attempt to reproduce the popular Chinese porcelain. The attempt failed, but Delft potters did succeed in making a white tin-glazed earthenware that looked very similar. The difference between earthenware and porcelain can be seen if the object is chipped: porcelain is white all through; earthenware is yellow or red. Earthenware production at Delft flourished in the second half of the 17th century and the first half of the 18th century. There were 25 factories at that time.

Through the inscription 'viva oranie' and the arms of Prince William III of Orange, the owner of this inkstand made clear his political allegiance. It is a typical product of the 1670s. At that time there were two sides: those who supported the States General and opposed the prince's appointment as stadholder, and those who were in favour of it.

Inkstand

faience, with a silver mounting

c. 1670-1680

15 x 21.5 x 13 cm

Bust of Prince William III of Orange as king of Great Britain
DELFTWARE FACTORY DE METALE POT
faience, c. 1695-1700
h. 42 cm

Bust of Mary II Stuart
DELFTWARE FACTORY DE GRIEKSCHE A
faience, c. 1680-1685
h. 32 cm

William III and his English wife Mary Stuart were popular in the Republic. Souvenirs of the couple were much in demand, even more so after they were crowned king and queen of England in 1689.
Mary was an avid collector of delftware. The palaces in the Netherlands and England were full of it. There were golden opportunities for the faience industry in Delft because large orders were also placed by those in court circles, royal houses abroad and wealthy citizens.
These busts come from different factories. 'De Metale Pot' was the only pottery to employ its own sculptor. Indeed, the bust of William is richer in form that that of Mary, which was probably made before she became queen of England. Unlike her husband, she is not wearing a crown.

Mary's passion for Chinese porcelain and delftware was rather excessive according to Daniel Defoe writing in the early 18th century: 'The queen brought in the custom or humour, as I may call it, of furnishing houses with china-ware, which increased to a strange degree afterwards, piling their china upon the tops of cabinets, scrutores, and every chimneypiece, to the tops of the ceilings...till it became a grievance in the expense of it.'

Shoe

faience, c. 1660-1675

8.5 x 15.5 cm

We can only guess as to what the function of this shoe might have been. Perhaps it was intended as a joke or as a light-hearted gift, with a nod to the erotic significance that shoes can have. At any rate it was a type of object that was popular until late in the 18th century. They were made in all shapes and sizes. The model here is a traditional Dutchman's shoe of around 1670. It is decorated with Chinese floral motifs.

Violin

faience, c. 1705-1710

63 x 22 cm

Even more exceptional is this violin with its virtuoso decorations. They are appropriate scenes to do with music. On the front elegant figures dance to the music of an orchestra; on the back peasants dance to the music of a fiddler. The maker of this violin wanted above all to demonstrate his skills, because it could not of course be played.

Teapot

DELFTWARE FACTORY

HET MORIAENSHOOFT

faience, c. 1685-1690

17.2 x 18.5 cm

Besides collector's items, a great deal of sumptuous ware was produced, from plates and jugs to complete services. But it is doubtful whether this teapot was ever used. It was probably meant to be purely decorative. It must have been a costly piece, because making an angular form was not easy. Moreover, it was painted in several colours, which was also time-consuming and very new at the time. For the deer and the other decorations the painter has drawn his inspiration from Chinese porcelain.

Tea drinking quickly became popular after the first large shipment of tea had been imported in 1667. In the early years it was very expensive and was brewed in small pots imported from China and imitated in Delft. Tea was mixed with hot water before being drunk.

Taking their lead from Japanese and Chinese polychrome porcelain, the delftware makers began to paint their products in several colours. The Hoppesteijn family were the first to do so around 1680. Production in several colours was labour-intensive. Blue and green fused with the white glaze during firing. Red and gold were added afterwards and fired at a lower temperature.

DELFTWARE

The sumptuous style that appealed to William and Mary is seen beautifully in these unusually large tiles. The abundant, symmetrically arranged decoration is typical of the French Louis XIV style that set the tone in William and Mary's circle. These tiles probably come from the Water Gallery at Hampton Court, the palace near London that was their favourite. When it was remodelled, the pavilion on the Thames was turned into private quarters for Mary. The walls were lined with these tiles, placed in sets of four one above the other. Together with Mary's collection of Chinese porcelain and delftware, which were also housed in the pavilion, it must have been an impressive ensemble.

Parts of a tile wall from the Water Gallery at Hampton Court

DELFTWARE FACTORY DE GRIEKSCHE A

faience, c. 1690

62 x 61.5 cm

The female figure is Fame. On one of her trumpets hangs a flag with a crown and William's monogram RWR.

Cherubs with a laurel wreath to adorn the bust of the king.

These tulip vases delight the eye, especially when they are full of colourful flowers. The pyramids stand one metre high and consist of seven separate vases of decreasing size stacked one on top of the other. A rod in the middle holds them together. This is a refined design somewhere between an Egyptian obelisk and a Chinese pagoda. The lavish decoration also reveals a mixture of influences.

The spectacular flower pyramids show better than anything else how daring Delft products could be around 1700. Such large pieces were eminently suitable for giving rooms an air of dignity. They are examples of princely display that were highly coveted in circles close to the court.

There was also a practical reason for having the pyramid consist of separate components. It would have been quite impossible around 1700 to fire such an enormous structure in one piece. There was a good chance that the vase would sag on one side or collapse in the hot kiln.

Flower holder in the form of a stacked obelisk

DELFTWARE FACTORY DE METALE POT

faience, c. 1710-1720

h. 101 cm

In the 17th century they were called 'flower pots with spouts'; now they are known as tulip vases. This suggests that in the past they were only used for tulips, but in fact other kinds of flowers were put in them. One in each spout, 4 per tier, so 36 in total.

ATTRIBUTED TO **JAN VAN MEKEREN** 1658-1733

Making marquetry was a time-consuming business. The tulip, for example, is made from two contrasting types of wood. Placed one on top of the other, they were sawn according to the pattern. After that, two tulips could be put together, with the colour contrast reversed in the second one, which was then used in another piece of furniture.

Bright yellow barberry, an indigenous type, was used for the sunflower. The colour is now a softer tint. The shadow on the left was obtained by scorching the wood in hot sand.

The tulip is made from two sorts of wood: the light wood is holly, the purplish kind is purplewood. It was imported from Brazil. The dark wood in the background is ebony from India.

Cabinet

ATTRIBUTED TO **JAN VAN MEKEREN**

oak, kingwood, ebony, rosewood, olivewood, maple, c. 1700

205 x 173 x 61 cm

The fritillary is made of purplewood and barberry. This flower was very popular in the 17th century. It often had a prominent position in painted bouquets too.

You could call it painting with wood, this new French fashion for decorating furniture with bouquets made up of hundreds of pieces of wood. They are pieces of veneer consisting of various woods and sawn to a pattern: native varieties like holly and barberry, but also exotic rosewood and ebony. They were glued to the cabinet. The woods were chosen for their colour and line patterns; where necessary colour was added. Thus all the leaves were stained green and the flowers red now and again. It must have been a colourful sight in the past, but now all that has faded. Yet the flowers can still be identified: fritillary, rose, sunflower and tulip.

The refined 'floral marquetry', as this technique developed in Paris is known, is probably the work of the Amsterdam cabinet-maker Jan van Mekeren. He specialized in this field. Here the technique has been applied to a typically Dutch piece of furniture, a cabinet on high legs joined by a stretcher. This simple form ensures that the ingenious decoration gets all the attention.

Holly was used for the lily.

The goldfinch consists of four types of wood: walnut (body); ebony (the tail and elsewhere); holly (breast); purplewood (bill). The table top is rosewood.

The rose consists entirely of holly. Colour was added with a red stain. The seams provide the line pattern.

CONSOLE TABLE AND GUÉRIDONS

Two guéridons
limewood, gilded, c. 1700
h. 146 cm

Console table with the four seasons
limewood, oak, gilded, c. 1700
87.5 x 108.5 x 73.5 cm

The console table and guéridons (candlestands) do not belong together, but are related in style. The figures are the eye-catching feature: at the top they have a human appearance and at the bottom they are standards. They bear the weight, as it were, of the table-top and the plateaus for the candlestands. All four of the turned female and male figures of the console table are different. A close look reveals that they represent the four seasons. They are identified by the fruits of their season. The classical style in which these pieces are made is characteristic of the designs of Daniel Marot. He played a leading part in the introduction of the style of the French court to the Netherlands and England. Before entering the service of William III in 1686, he worked for the French king. No one was more up to date with the latest fashions and customs at the French court.

Most of the original gilding has been lost. The appearance of the table is now dominated by the red-brown ground, which was applied before the gilt. The effect was to give the gold a warmer glow.

MELCHIOR D'HONDECOETER 1636-1695

A pelican and other birds near a pool, known as 'The floating feather'
MELCHIOR D'HONDECOETER
oil on canvas, c. 1680
159 x 144 cm

A white feather floats in a pond. It is so convincingly done that the painting soon came to be known as 'The floating feather'.
Melchior d'Hondecoeter specialized in 'bird pieces'. His patrons were mainly rich Amsterdam merchants and regents. The monumental paintings were well suited to the stately interiors of their mansions. William III was also an admirer of Hondecoeter, whose work could be found in three of the ruler's palaces. 'The floating feather' was probably done for Het Loo Palace at Apeldoorn.

Hondecoeter painted the birds from life. He had his own poultry yard, but he would have studied more exotic species in the aviaries at country houses. William III had aviaries at his palaces and in one case an extensive menagerie. It is said that Hondecoeter had trained a cock to stand still on command. This tall story was meant to indicate how true to life Hondecoeter's birds were.

The white feather.

PAINTING

NEW PAINTING

Paintings were popular in the Golden Age. They could be found in every home, whether it was lived in by the ruling elite, the middle class or country folk. Not only were a great many produced, but there was also a wide range of genres, to suit every taste and purse. The variety and the high degree of specialization were distinctive aspects. There were painters who only did portraits. Others concentrated on depicting everyday scenes or specialized in still lifes. Some chose landscape as their subject and within that field there were again specializations, such as the winter landscape.

• pages 76-81

HAARLEM, CENTRE OF ART

In the early 17th century Haarlem was one of the leading Dutch cities. A wealthy commercial centre, it was celebrated for the production of fine linen cloths and had a high reputation in the field of art. Haarlem was the cradle of Dutch landscape painting and of the 'banquet', as still lifes with 'laid tables' were then known. This genre evolved from an artificial display of objects into an ever more natural-looking depiction. In the work of Heda the illusion of reality is almost complete. Haarlem was also where Pieter Saenredam painted his architectural views and Frans Hals his matchless portraits.

• pages 82-91

THE ATTRACTION OF AMSTERDAM

The spectacular growth of Amsterdam into a centre of world trade and its consequent affluence made it hugely attractive to painters. At the beginning of the 17th century they were mainly Flemish; later on most of them had already made their name elsewhere but hoped to become rich in Amsterdam. Rembrandt was one of them, just like his pupils and the portraitist Bartholomeus van der Helst. Amsterdam offered greater opportunities: the market was bigger and there was also the prospect of making international contacts.

• pages 92-99

IN FULL BLOOM

The 1650s and 1660s might be called the 'pinnacle of painting'. This was the great age of landscape, still life and portraiture. Everything was possible and could be made even finer, stronger or subtler. In this period Jan Both and his colleagues painted their majestic Italian landscapes, Albert Cuyp revealed the poetic aspects of Dutch river landscapes and Jacob van Ruisdael captured their grandeur. The still-life painters perfected their technique even further and the great Rembrandt painted his peerless masterpieces.

• pages 100-109

REMBRANDT

Rembrandt van Rijn is without doubt the most celebrated painter of the Golden Age. He was born in 1606 in Leiden, where he began his own workshop some twenty years later. In 1631 he moved to Amsterdam, quickly making a name for himself because of his dramatic painting style and strong contrasts between light and dark. The self-portraits show us how he developed as a painter and how he gradually aged. He did a whole series of them: in total he must have sat before the mirror some eighty times to record his features, in paintings, etchings and drawings. As a result, his appearance is also better known to us than that of any other 17th-century figure.

• pages 92-96; 106-109

Winter landscapes with skaters
HENDRICK AVERCAMP
oil on panel, c. 1608
77.3 x 131.9 cm

HENDRICK AVERCAMP 1585-1634

It is the depths of winter: the canal is frozen over, the trees are bare, the houses are covered in snow. Smoke curls from a chimney and the people are warmly wrapped up. It must be cold, but not cold enough to stay at home. The ice brings out the crowds: young and old, rich and poor, country people and town dwellers.

Hendrick Avercamp was one of the first specialists. He became the master of the Dutch winter view with broad expanses of ice, snow-filled skies and merry ice sports. They were known in the 17th century as 'Wintertjes'. Avercamp was deaf and mute, but despite this he became a born storyteller. He depicted the hundreds of figures with a fine eye for detail: the skaters, one occasionally falling, children riding on a sledge, a horse sleigh, 'kolf' or golf players, and well-off citizens in conversation. But he also painted poor wretches. For them it is a day like any other. They haul cane and fish, break a hole in the ice, draw water or beg.

There is much to discover in this painting: a pair of lovers in the haystack, a peasant relieving himself in the privy (a boat turned on its side). This was entirely normal among peasants at the time. But for the buyers – the 'civilized' townspeople – such anecdotes were highly amusing.

ESAIAS VAN DE VELDE 1587-1630

The ferry
ESAIAS VAN DE VELDE
oil on panel, 1622
75.5 x 113 cm

Green lowlands, a straight horizon, clouds and water. It is a typical Dutch river landscape that is revealed here, with rowing boats and a ferry. The crossing is beautifully caught: passengers, cows and a horse and cart on a barge that is poled across by ferrymen while people stand waiting at the water's edge on both sides. But the viewer's gaze wanders, zigzagging over the water, towards a boat yard with a sailing boat and from there to a church and a windmill which are reflected in the water. Esaias van de Velde painted this remarkable river view in 1622. It is a masterpiece in which the tranquil, rustic atmosphere of the Dutch countryside is perfectly captured. He was the first painter to portray the beauty of Holland in a large format. With 'The cattle ferry' he set the tone for a long tradition of Dutch river views.

JOHANNES TORRENTIUS 1589-1644

Emblematic still life with flagon, glass, jug and bridle
JOHANNES TORRENTIUS
oil on panel, 1614
diameter 51/51.5 cm

A shelf with drinking vessels, two clay pipes, a music sheet and in the background a bridle. A rather curious combination which only becomes clear when one reads the verse: 'wat buten maat bestaat, int onmaats quaat verghaat'. In other words, those who know no moderation come to a bad end. The objects allude to 'keeping measure': a bridle is used to curb a horse, while the wine flagon, glass and water jug together represent moderation. After all, it is advisable to mix wine with water.

Ironically, the painter of this masterpiece, Torrentius, was himself anything but moderate. In 1628 he was sentenced to twenty years in the house of correction for 'heresy and polygamy' and much of his work was publicly burned. Two years later he was released on the intercession of Charles I of England, once the owner of this still life.

This is the only known painting by Torrentius. In 1913 it was found by chance in an attic, where it was being used as a lid on a tub of currants.

According to Constantijn Huygens, a contemporary, Torrentius was 'a wonder in depicting lifeless objects'. He doubted whether anyone else would be able 'to portray objects of glass, pewter, earthenware and iron, which have a certain kind of lustre and which up to now have been thought too difficult for the brush, with so much expression and such subtle beauty'.

WERNER VAN DEN VALCKERT c. 1585-1627/28

Portrait of a man with ring and touchstone, probably Bartholomeus Jansz van Assendelft (1585-1658)
WERNER VAN DEN VALCKERT
oil on panel, 1617
66 x 49.5 cm

The identity of the sitter in this lively portrait was long a mystery. These days he is believed to be Bartholomeus Jansz van Assendelft, a goldsmith of Leiden. The ring he shows and the black stone under his left hand provided the solution. They allude to Van Assendelft's profession of assayer. The stone is a touchstone used to test gold and silver. The purity of precious metal could be established by rubbing it over the stone. Van Assendelft was made assay master of the guild of gold- and silversmiths in 1617. It was the first office he held – a good reason for having his portrait painted. The Leiden goldsmith turned to the Amsterdam portraitist Van den Valckert rather than to a fellow townsman, and this proved to be no bad choice. This unusual, almost photographic portrait is refined, elegant and yet animated.

Van den Valckert put his name and the year on the touchstone.

HENDRICK DE KEYSER 1565-1621

Bust of Vincent Jacobsz Coster
HENDRICK DE KEYSER
marble, 1608
h. 75 cm

Vincent Coster is dressed in a classical toga in this portrait sculpted by Hendrick de Keyser. This was the first time that a Dutch burgher had had himself immortalized in marble. Previously, only the nobility had done that. Coster was a rich man. He had earned his fortune as a 'wine gauger', responsible for gauging the content of casks and calculating the excise duty. His nickname was 'Centen Peijlder' (Cents Gauger). He also derived income from the Oude Doolhof, a pleasure garden on Prinsengracht in Amsterdam. It is known that there were marble sculptures by De Keyser in this garden.

The choice of a toga shows how this Amsterdammer wanted to be seen – as a Roman statesman. The costume gives the portrait a dignified air, but the pose and the realistic features ensure that it has liveliness. De Keyser captured them unerringly.

DIRCK HALS 1591-1656

The fête champêtre
DIRCK HALS
oil on panel, 1627
77.6 x 135.7 cm

A lively garden party is taking place in the park of a stylish country house. A group of dandies and their ladies are enjoying themselves eating, drinking, flirting and making music. Sensual pleasure seems to be the sole object, but the painter unobtrusively gives a subtle warning. He does this by means of the chained monkey. It stands for man, who lets himself be fettered by his sins and cannot free himself. In this way the viewer is warned not to let celebrating degenerate into licentiousness.

Dirck Hals gives a superb picture of the extravagant fashions of the 1620s, but in depicting the villa and garden he is less realistic. Country houses in the Netherlands were still quite modest up to 1650.

Dirck Hals was ten years younger than his brother Frans, from whom he probably learned his craft. Yet there are few similarities between the brothers' paintings. Dirck mainly painted merry, colourful 'companies', while Frans was a portraitist.

JUDITH LEYSTER 1600/10-1660

The serenade
JUDITH LEYSTER
oil on panel, 1629
45.5 x 35 cm

Judith Leyster did not paint a great deal, but what she did paint more than repays attention: for example, this lute player strumming his instrument in a serenade. Completely lost in his music, he directs his gaze upward in rapture. He is shown from close up and from below. This gives the scene the air of a snapshot, as if he has been caught out while playing. The strong lighting adds to this effect.

Judith Leyster was one of the few 17th-century women to have earned her living by painting. Her work is related to that of her Haarlem contemporary Frans Hals. Both share a fluent painting style and a preference for merry types. Judith set up practice as an independent artist in 1629. She gave up painting when she married the painter Jan Miense Molenaer in 1636.

Beatrix was 30 when she married Isaac, who was 35. He was an interesting, cultivated man. At the age of 13 he had been sent to Moscow to be taught by merchants there. He spent eight years in the country and became fluent in Russian. In addition to being a merchant, he was a diplomat, historian and cartographer. Isaac no doubt advised the artist on portraying the symbolic plants.

Wedding portrait of Isaac Abrahamsz Massa and Beatrix van der Laen

FRANS HALS

oil on canvas, c. 1622

140 x 166.5 cm

FRANS HALS 1581-1666

It was rare in the 17th century for people to be shown beaming and relaxed the way Isaac Massa and Beatrix van der Laen are here. He was a wealthy Haarlem merchant and she the daughter of a burgomaster. They were married on 26 April 1622 and not long afterwards Frans Hals painted this unusual wedding portrait. Married couples generally had themselves portrayed looking dignified and earnest, and as a rule separately. This couple wanted something different and had themselves painted in a garden, side by side, in love and spontaneously smiling at the artist. Beatrix proudly shows her wedding ring, Isaac has his hand on his heart. The portrait rather resembles a snapshot, as if Hals had caught the couple in the garden and 'taken a picture'. The figures are done fluently, almost nonchalantly. Only the faces, ruffs and cuffs are depicted with greater precision.

It was a stroke of genius to use the garden as the setting for the wedding portrait. Hals was thus able to add some plants which look ordinary at first sight but here have a special meaning. The thistle next to Isaac was then known as 'husband's fidelity', while the ivy beside Beatrix symbolizes love and devotion. The vine winding around the tree is also a symbol of love and friendship. Even the garden has meaning. It is a 17th-century variant of the medieval garden of love.

The garden of love: here the fountain is the source of love.

It is not known whom Frans Hals has depicted so vividly here. Is it a portrait or just a painting of a drunken man intended for the free market? Drinkers were portrayed quite often in the 17th century, mostly as types in curious get-ups. But Hals's drinker is wearing 17th-century dress and is so true to life that he could step out of the frame at any moment.

Frans Hals is known for his virtuoso style of painting. 'The merry drinker' is one of the most famous examples of this. Forms are suggested by vigorous, broad brushstrokes and a couple of rapid accents. The glass, for instance, consists of just a few black lines and a little white for the reflection. Even more extraordinary is the tangle of lines that only becomes a lace collar when seen from a distance. Hals's painting manner is so fluent that for a time the work was thought to be unfinished.

A civic guardsman holding a berkemeijer, known as 'The merry drinker'
FRANS HALS
oil on canvas
c. 1628-1630
81 x 66.5 cm

JOHANNES VERSPRONCK 1597-1662

Portrait of a girl dressed in blue
JOHANNES VERSPRONCK
oil on canvas, 1641
82 x 66.5 cm

She must be about ten years old, this girl in blue. Yet she looks like an adult woman. This is due to her clothing. In the past children were dressed just like their parents from as early as the age of five or six. Only the face reveals the age: bright eyes and a bloom on the cheeks.
It is not known who the girl is. All the signs suggest that she comes from a privileged background. She is dressed according to the latest fashion in a roundly bulging gown adorned with gold braid and accessories in fine linen and Flemish bobbin lace: a jabot, a collar, a neckerchief around the shoulders, and cuffs. Jewellery and a fashionable feather fan complete the ensemble.

Without collar and cuffs the 17th-century burgher was not dressed. The Dutch prided themselves on the fine quality of their linen and foreign visitors noticed this too. As early as the end of the 16th century, an Englishman claimed that 'nowhere else in the world are such fine shirts' worn as in Holland.

FLORIS VAN DIJCK 1575-1651

Still life with cheeses
FLORIS VAN DIJCK
oil on panel, c. 1615
82.5 x 111.4 cm

The most eye-catching things on this table are the stacked Dutch cheeses. The creamy yellow of the young cheese is reflected in the pewter plate. Around it are displayed dishes with fruit, glasses, a flagon, some bread and nuts – all everyday items with an occasional expensive piece, such as the Chinese porcelain or the damask napkin.
But the still-life painter was not concerned with that. What mattered to him was to depict the different materials as realistically as possible: transparent glass, wafer-thin porcelain, stone, reflecting pewter, the dull shine of apples and pears, juicy grapes, crunchy bread crusts and smoothly ironed damask. This is why Floris van Dijck depicted the table as viewed from above and arranged the objects so that they are all seen to best advantage.

PIETER CLAESZ 1596/97-1660

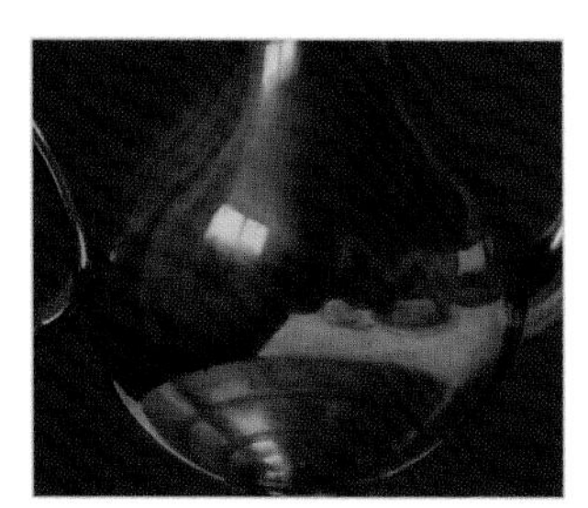

Part of the table and a window are reflected in the flagon.

Still life with turkey pie
PIETER CLAESZ
oil on panel, 1627
76.5 x 135 cm

Claesz went a step further: his laid table is set in a room. The objects are again chosen for their texture, but also now to show off, as with the expensive turkey pie or the sliced lemon. Salt and pepper – costly items at that time – are prominently displayed (in a rolled-up page from an almanac).

WILLEM CLAESZ HEDA 1594-1680

Still life with gilt goblet

WILLEM CLAESZ HEDA

oil on panel, 1635

88 x 113 cm

This looks like the remains of a banquet, but is in fact a carefully considered composition. Heda has arranged the objects so that he can give the best possible demonstration of his skills. This is why the drinking vessel is lying on its side, so that both the dull silver under the foot and the gleaming exterior can be seen. It is an absolute tour de force. Because the objects are depicted one behind the other rather than being seen from above, the composition looks more natural than that of its predecessors. The sublime rendition of materials and reflections adds to this effect.

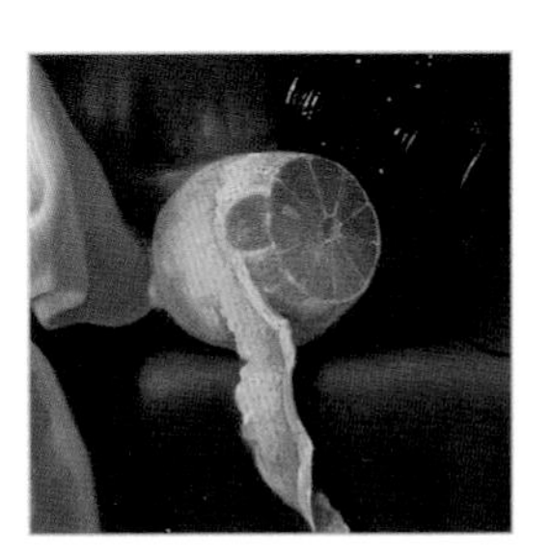

The yellow of the lemon gives some colour to this monochrome painting.

Putting the plate on the edge of the table serves to suggest depth.

Cheese was one of the principal Dutch exports. In a poem Jacob Cats compared the successful dairy industry with the lemon imported from Spain. It could only be picked once a year, whereas 'what the cow provides is richer treasure / For twice a day it gives the noble fluid'.

Interior of the St. Odulphus Church in Assendelft

PIETER SAENREDAM

oil on panel, 1649

49.6 x 75 cm

When in 1628 Pieter Saenredam decided to specialize in painting architecture, he opted to depict existing buildings. This was something new at that time. He painted church buildings primarily and enjoyed great success from the start.

Saenredam had already been living in Haarlem for forty years when he painted the 'portrait' of the church in his native village of Assendelft. His father and two relatives were buried there. Their names are inscribed on the gravestone in the right foreground, making this church interior a tribute to his forefathers.

This is a Protestant church with no frills. People are listening to the sermon – diminutive figures in an overwhelming space. Painting the portrait of the building was a lengthy process. In the case of the St. Odulphus Church, it took no less than sixteen years. Saenredam made the first sketches in 1633 and 1634. On the basis of them and of exact measurements, in 1643 he made the perspective construction. It laid the foundation for this masterly painting, which was finished on 2 October 1649, as can be read on the pew on the left.

Of the St. Odulphus Church only the gravestone has survived. In translation the Latin text reads: 'Here lie the earthly remains of Jan Saenredam, the very celebrated engraver, Petrus the Younger, sheriff of Assendelft for forty-four years, his son Gerard de Jonge, doctor in secular and church law and advocate.'

PIETER SAENREDAM 1597-1665

In 1641 Saenredam travelled to Amsterdam to draw the old town hall on the Dam. It took him six full days. It was not by chance that he did this, for in 1640 it had been decided to replace the medieval complex of four buildings by a new town hall, one which was better suited to the image of the world's leading commercial centre (see page 13).
Saenredam made this painting in 1657 on the basis of his earlier drawing. The old town hall had been destroyed by fire five years earlier 'in no longer than three hours' time'. He recorded this on the plinth of the building.
Saenredam's painting was bought by the burgomasters of Amsterdam in 1658 for the burgomaster's chamber in the new town hall (now the Royal Palace), which by then had already been in use for three years. Saenredam received 400 guilders for it.

The old town hall of Amsterdam

PIETER SAENREDAM

oil on panel, 1657

65.5 x 84.5 cm

Self-portrait at an early age

REMBRANDT HARMENSZ VAN RIJN

oil on panel, c. 1628

22.6 x 18.7 cm

Rembrandt was about 22 when he painted this self-portrait. It is one of the first, and he was at the beginning of his career. It is a daring portrait, for the larger part of his face is in shadow. Only the neck, ear lobe, part of the cheek and a bit of the nose catch the light. In fact it is not a true portrait, but rather a study in which Rembrandt experimented with light and shade.

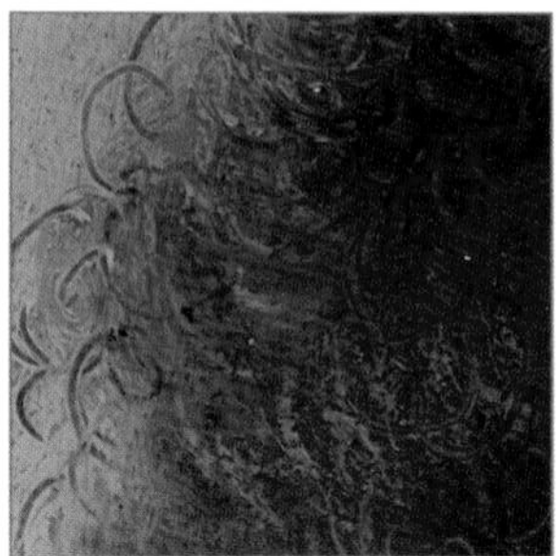

Rembrandt suggested the curls by scratching in the paint while it was still wet, so that the colours underneath were revealed.

REMBRANDT VAN RIJN 1606-1669

Self-portrait as the apostle Paul

REMBRANDT HARMENSZ VAN RIJN

oil on canvas, 1661

91 x 77 cm

Thick layers of paint – applied wet into wet – suggest the various layers of fabric.

Many of Rembrandt's self-portraits were bought by visitors to his workshop as highly coveted demonstrations of his abilities.

It was entirely normal in the 17th century for artists to be visited in their workshop. A Frenchman wrote in a guide for art lovers (1635): 'You must have visited the workshop, held discussions with the masters, seen the magical effects of their brush...'

Rembrandt's self-portraits are fascinating, in part because he presents himself in the most diverse roles. Here the 55-year-old artist uses his own appearance to portray the apostle Paul, one of Christ's twelve disciples. Paul is identified by the sword under his arm, his normal attribute. The turban is a reference to his oriental origins, while the papers allude to the epistles he wrote.

Rembrandt was very interested in the figure of Paul, who as the preacher of the Christian faith was popular among both Catholics and Protestants. He depicted him several times. This fluently painted portrait with a pensive, slightly surprised look is the most expressive version.

According to the Bible, Jeremia predicted to the king of Judah that Jerusalem would be destroyed if the king did not grant the wishes of his opponent. Jeremia's prediction came true: the city was taken and set on fire. And the king was blinded.
Rembrandt summarizes this story in this painting with the one grieving figure dramatically lit against a dark background. In the distance on the left there is a glimpse of the burning city and an army. The blind king can also be discerned. He is standing by the steps with his fists pressed against his eyes.
Rembrandt painted this work in 1630, his last year in Leiden. He was to move to Amsterdam the year afterwards. The 'Jeremiah' is an early masterpiece. The contrast between the figure done in elaborate detail, and the objects beside him, and the much more roughly painted background is superb.

Jeremia lamenting the destruction of Jerusalem
REMBRANDT HARMENSZ VAN RIJN
oil on panel, 1630
58.3 x 46.6 cm

Portrait of Johannes Wtenbogaert
REMBRANDT HARMENSZ VAN RIJN
oil on canvas, 1633
130 x 103 cm

Rembrandt had not been living in Amsterdam for very long when he painted this portrait of the minister Johannes Wtenbogaert, one of Holland's most important religious leaders. It was not intended for the minister himself but for one of his supporters, the Amsterdam merchant Abraham Recht. The commission must have been an honour for the young Rembrandt: he was then 26, while Wtenbogaert was 76. Rembrandt produced an imposing and animated portrait. It is as if the minister looks up from his studies and turns to the viewer. The lighting draws our attention to the wrinkled face with the lively but old, slightly moist eyes. The snow-white ruff stands out strongly against the brown fur coat and the black suit. On the left Rembrandt recorded the minister's age.

As the leader of the liberal movement, Johannes Wtenbogaert (1557-1644) was an advocate of tolerance within the Reformed Church. When the strict Calvinists gained the ascendancy in 1617, Wtenbogaert was exiled. He returned to the Netherlands in 1626.

Portrait of Maria Trip
REMBRANDT HARMENSZ VAN RIJN
oil on panel, 1639
107 x 82 cm

Rembrandt soon made a name for himself in Amsterdam as a portrait painter. Leading families were among his patrons, including the rich Trip family of merchants. Maria was twenty years old and still unmarried when Rembrandt painted her. Whether this portrait was intended as a visiting card for a potential suitor is not known, but Rembrandt made Maria as attractive as possible: she is richly adorned with jewels, and her clothes and hairstyle are in the latest French fashion. Two years later she married the wealthy merchant Balthasar Coymans.

As was the custom for women of her rank, Maria is wearing a black gown. It falls open to reveal the petticoat decorated with gold lace. Over her shoulders she has a collar and neckerchief trimmed with costly lace. The folding fan in her hand, the latest thing from China, was also expensive.

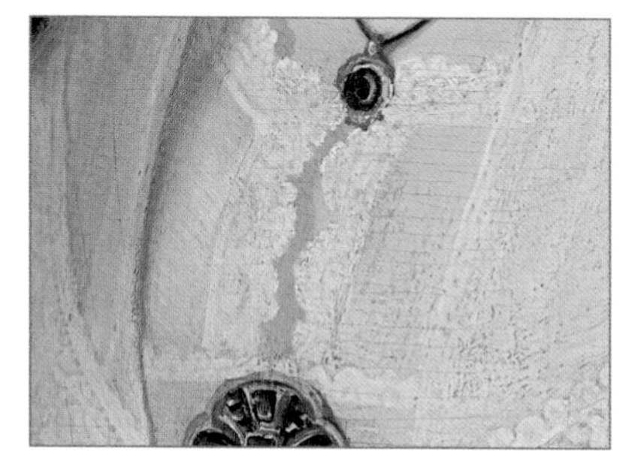

Showing the décolleté was not fitting. Only ladies at court did that. Commoners covered the décolleté with a semi-transparent cloth known as a 'neerstick' or jabot.

BARTHOLOMEUS VAN DER HELST 1613-1670

Portrait of Gerard Bicker

BARTHOLOMEUS VAN DER HELST

oil on panel, 1642

94 x 70.5 cm

Portrait of Andries Bicker

BARTHOLOMEUS VAN DER HELST

oil on panel, 1642

93.5 x 70.5 cm

Bartholomeus van der Helst, who moved to Amsterdam in 1637, was soon competing with Rembrandt as a portraitist of the leading families. In 1642, when Van der Helst painted these portraits, the Bicker family was the most powerful in the city. Andries Bicker was a merchant in the Russian trade and held numerous administrative offices. The fact that he gave Van der Helst the commission for the family portraits tells us something about the painter's abilities. His style of painting was evidently well liked.

Father and son are shown in the same pose, self-assured, with one hand at the waist. With his black clothes and pleated ruff, the father makes a forceful impression. This contrasts with the son in his fashionable suit. Because of his voluminous girth, he appears less resolute. Van der Helst also painted the mother. That portrait is in Dresden.

AERT VAN DER NEER 1603/04-1677

River view by moonlight

AERT VAN DER NEER

oil on panel, c. 1645

55 x 103 cm

The story goes that Aert van der Neer thought painting a landscape by moonlight was not that difficult: with a little brown, black, blue, yellow and white you could create the atmosphere in no time. The truth was rather different. Van der Neer developed his speciality gradually.

In all its simplicity this river view is a marvel. Moonlight colours the clouds and the water, in which the surroundings are reflected. It shines on the house fronts, the cattle and the boats on the river. Here and there only silhouettes can be discerned. To achieve certain light effects Van der Neer occasionally used technical tricks. For instance, he scratched in the wet paint and also used his fingers. However beautiful his 'moonlights' were, Van der Neer received little for them. He had to earn extra income as an innkeeper and eventually went bankrupt.

The fence was scratched into the wet paint, leaving the light ground visible.

One of the places with a fingerprint.

JAN VAN GOYEN 1596-1656

Two old oaks stand out against the grey sky. Beneath them two travellers rest. To the left unfolds a panorama with a town on a river. A third figure is on his way to the town. In this landscape by Jan van Goyen the red and blue jackets of the travellers are the only colour accents. But these men were not the painter's main concern. What mattered to him above all were the curiously shaped oaks, the space and the atmosphere. He captured that through a sophisticated composition and a loose, direct manner of painting, and by using only a few colours – green, grey, yellow and brown in many shades. This also enabled him to work quickly, and cheaply. Van Goyen was exceptionally productive. He made some 800 drawings and 1200 paintings, often reusing successful compositions so that he could keep up this high output. This group of oaks, for example, is seen elsewhere in his oeuvre, as is the river panorama.

Landscape with two oaks

JAN VAN GOYEN

oil on canvas, 1641

88.5 x 110.5 cm

Around 1627 Van Goyen began painting monochrome landscapes. That is to say that he confined himself to a few – closely related – colours.

Italian landscape with draughtsman

JAN BOTH

oil on canvas, c. 1650

187 x 240 cm

JAN BOTH

c. 1615-1652

Several men have sat down in the shade by a mountain stream. One of them is drawing a sketch and a ray of sunlight shines on the paper. Another chats to one of the herdsmen grazing his goats here. To the right there is a sun-baked panorama with mountains.

Jan Both painted this Italian landscape in Utrecht, many years after his period in Rome. He went there because, like a number of his colleagues, he had come under the spell of the Italian landscape. Even when they were back in their native country, these other painters also went on producing southern landscapes, always bathed in warm sunlight and enlivened by herdsmen and travellers. The drawings they had once done on the spot in Italy served as aids to memory. Both is regarded as one of the most important Italianate painters, as these artists are known. His work was popular in the highest circles and fetched good prices. This unusually imposing landscape must have been rather expensive.

AELBERT CUYP 1620-1691

River landscape with riders

AELBERT CUYP

oil on canvas, c. 1655

128 x 227.5 cm

Two riders break off their journey briefly at a river to let their horses drink. It is late afternoon, the setting sun shines on the clouds from the side and casts a golden glow over the land. The warm, listless mood makes the river view seem un-Dutch, almost southern. Yet this is part of the Netherlands, namely the hilly area along the Rhine between Nijmegen and Kleve. Aelbert Cuyp journeyed there from his home in Dordrecht in 1652. The drawings he made then inspired this idyllic river landscape with an Arcadian atmosphere.

Dutch landscapes, cows and horses were the subjects that Cuyp preferred to depict, always bathed in a golden light. He borrowed that from the painters of Italian landscapes, such as Jan Both. Cuyp himself was never in Italy.

JACOB VAN RUISDAEL 1628/29-1682

The windmill at Wijk bij Duurstede

JACOB VAN RUISDAEL

oil on canvas, c. 1670

83 x 101 cm

Never before had a windmill been depicted with such mastery as in this painting. Mills were a common sight in the Golden Age; there were thousands of them. But Ruisdael saw their beauty and brought it out in this dramatically lit landscape.

Ruidael is the undisputed master of the Dutch landscape. He generally depicted imaginary views, but this picture of the mill at Wijk bij Duurstede is reasonably reliable in its topography: the town's truncated church tower still stands. The castle on the left has since disappeared. But Ruisdael did give himself some licence when portraying the mill in its setting.

The miller and three women.

He showed the mill as seen from underneath, so that the huge structure towers over the town. Moreover, he left out the city gate and put three women in its place. These diminutive figures serve to make the mill look even bigger.

JAN DAVIDSZ DE HEEM 1606 - c.1684

Festoon of fruits and flowers

JAN DAVIDSZ DE HEEM

oil on canvas, c. 1660

74 x 60 cm

This rich array of fruits is a feast for the eye. Yellow and blue plums, peaches, apricots, blackberries, cherries, grapes, a pomegranate and lemons: they are so deceptively real that you want to take hold of them. The fruits are interspersed with flowers, foliage, insects, butterflies and occasional ears of corn. A close look will also reveal a snail.

Despite the artificial combination, as a whole the work makes a natural impression. This is due mainly to De Heem's marvellous technique: from the soft skin of a peach to the dew on grapes or the lightly pocked rind of a lemon, everything is equally convincing.

De Heem's luxuriant fruit and flower still lifes found a ready market among the well-off, princes and rich citizens, who were often art lovers.

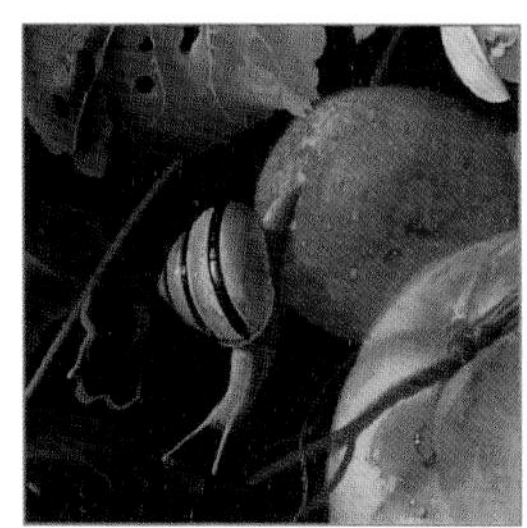

The public may have loved them, but among artists there was little appreciation for fruit and flower still lifes. Even if, like those by De Heem, they were 'taken to the point of deceiving'. One painter went so far as to call the genre 'feminine', in other words, art for women.

WILLEM KALF 1619-1693

While De Heem works magic with colour, Willem Kalf does the same with light. In the dark several costly objects catch the light. They are only visible in part, such as the dish of Chinese porcelain, the watch in front of it and the handle of a knife. The wine glass in the background is even harder to see. Only the silver jug and the lemons stand out.
The objects have been chosen mainly for their lustre. What mattered to Kalf were the reflections, for example of the lemons in the silver, in the gilt and in the glass. Still subtler is the reflection of the blue of the porcelain. Kalf's magical still lifes sold well. The watch would have been particularly prized. In the midst of all these showpieces, it is a reminder of the transience of life

Still life with silver jug

WILLEM KALF

oil on canvas, c. 1665

73.8 x 65.2 cm

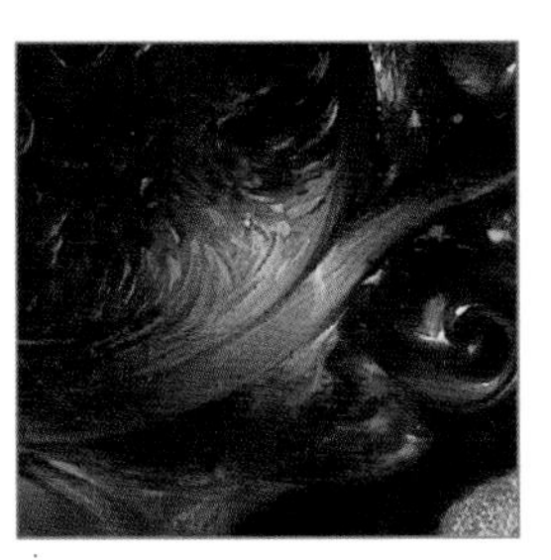

Both the jug and the holder for the glass are decorated with the popular auricular ornament. These are masterpieces of the silversmith's art made by Christiaen van Vianen (jug) and Johannes Lutma (holder).

Isaac and Rebecca, known as 'The Jewish bride'

REMBRANDT HARMENSZ VAN RIJN

oil on canvas, c. 1665

121.5 x 166.5 cm

Vincent van Gogh was lyrical when he saw Rembrandt's 'Jewish bride' in 1885. 'What an intimate, what an infinitely sympathetic painting,' he said to a friend. 'Believe me, and I mean this sincerely, I would give ten years of my life to be allowed to sit before this painting for fourteen days with just a crust of bread to eat.'

REMBRANDT VAN RIJN 1606-1669

The woman responds dreamily to her husband's caress. Rembrandt managed to put so much love and tenderness into that one gesture of her hand on his that it dominates the entire scene. It is so intimate that you feel an impulse to look away. This loving couple on a seat are the biblical Isaac and Rebecca. Rembrandt deliberately kept the setting vague – only a plant is visible – in order to concentrate on the couple. It is possible that contemporaries of Rembrandt had themselves portrayed as Isaac and Rebecca. In the 17th century people quite often had their portraits painted as biblical figures.

The manner in which Rembrandt depicted the couple is spectacular. He painted the faces and hands fairly smoothly. With the clothes, however, he went to work roughly, with daubs and thickly applied paint. This ensures that the painting catches more light at certain points, in the man's golden yellow sleeve, for instance, and in the red dress. Elsewhere Rembrandt scratched in the still wet paint, so that the light ground became visible.

Detail of the red dress.

Detail of the golden yellow sleeve.

Bronze green coat with scratches.

The syndics of the Amsterdam drapers' guild

REMBRANDT HARMENSZ VAN RIJN

oil on canvas, 1662

191.5 x 279 cm

The names of those portrayed are known. Surprisingly, they turn out to belong to different religious denominations. The sampling officials thus provide a good picture of the tolerant Amsterdam society of around 1660. At the beginning of the 17th century administrative offices were held solely by Protestants.

As if they are just pausing in their work to see who is entering – that is how Rembrandt portrays the five sampling officials and their servant. The second man from the left rises from his chair and the man next to him seems to say something; the gesture of his hand suggests that he is speaking. From this Rembrandt created an extraordinarily absorbing portrait, because the person entering is in fact the viewer. In this way he involves the viewer and enlivens the portrait. The brilliant composition took a great deal of thought: research has shown that he first depicted the standing official in a sitting position, and that the servant – the only one without a hat – stood in various places.

The sitters are the sampling officials of the Amsterdam drapers' guild who monitored the quality of laken, a felt-like woollen cloth, in 1661 and 1662. To do this they used test pieces or samples for comparison, hence the name 'sampling officials'. The portrait was intended for the regents' chamber in the Staalhof, the Drapers' guildhall in Staalstraat. It was to be hung high up (above the chimneypiece), and Rembrandt took this into account by adjusting the perspective: we look at the table from below.

Rembrandt's signature and the year on the chimneypiece were added in the 18th century.

CONTINUATION **PAINTING**

PAINTING AT HOME AND ON THE STREET

The unique character of Dutch painting is best expressed in the depictions of scenes from everyday life. They are known as genre pieces and show people in their surroundings – at home, at work or in the tavern. Not only the rich, but the middle classes too.

Paintings of this kind were very popular in the 17th century. They give a good impression of life in the Republic: how people behaved, how they amused themselves, how they dressed, what preoccupied them, what they ate and drank. These scenes often look so natural that it is easy to forget that the artists composed them in their studios. Sometimes they contain a moralistic message. • pages 112-121

JOHANNES VERMEER

Johannes Vermeer is one of the most famous artists of the Golden Age. This was not always the case: in his own time he was known only to a small circle. A resident of Delft, he made a living by dealing in art as well as painting. This did not make him a rich man. Of the few paintings he produced, 35 have survived. • pages 112-116

MASTERS IN GENRES

In the second half of the Golden Age there were a number of renowned artists who specialized in one genre, in which they achieved impressive results. They clearly had a particular audience in mind. For example, Jan Steen, the master of humour, must have known that there was a market for comic paintings. The marine painters met the demand for atmospheric sea views, architecture painters depicted the city and livestock painters took the Dutch cow as their subject. • pages 122-131

CIVIC GUARD PORTRAITS

Anyone entering a civic guard building in the 17th century must have been overwhelmed by all the guards' portraits hung there. These paintings, 125 of which have been preserved, express an unmistakable civic pride. The civic guards belonged to the upper classes. A portrait of them was the most prestigious commission that a portraitist could obtain. It was a measure of his success. • pages 132-137

MASTERPIECES ON PAPER

The 17th century was also a Golden Age for Dutch drawings and prints as artists explored the visual world in their drawings. Painters such as Jan van Goyen and Albert Cuyp not only made landscape drawings in preparation for their paintings but also as works of art in their own right. Without question, the most talented and versatile of the Dutch artists was Rembrandt. He proved himself an unrivalled master in not only his drawings but also in his prints of landscapes, portraits and Biblical and mythological tableaus. • pages 138-139

WORK IN PROGRESS

The main building of the Rijksmuseum is currently undergoing extensive renovations to ensure it meets all the requirements of a modern museum. More than 7000 objects, soon to be displayed in eighty different halls, will cover the period from the late Middle Ages to present day. Paintings, sculptures, historical objects and the decorative arts covering more than six centuries of art and history will be on display in a building that is fit for the 21st century. • pages 140-141

The milkmaid

JOHANNES VERMEER

oil on canvas, c. 1658-1660

45.5 x 41 cm

JOHANNES VERMEER 1632-1675

'The kitchen maid' is one of Vermeer's most admired paintings. Standing next to a window, she pours milk into a bowl with careful concentration, her head at a slight angle. The fall of light automatically leads the viewer's gaze to the stream of milk. This is so magnificently rendered that you can almost see and hear it flowing. Nothing else happens in the room.

The simplicity of the subject is underlined by the sturdily built woman with her hands brown from work. She is dressed plainly but colourfully: a yellow bodice with green oversleeves, a red and a blue skirt. A sublime portrait of an ordinary maid. It is fascinating to see how Vermeer suggested reality. He paid attention to the smallest details: holes in the wall, a nail complete with shadow, a broken pane of glass. His rendering of the different materials is masterly. A close look reveals small highlights everywhere, sometimes mat, sometimes gleaming. There the paint is just a little thicker and so catches more light. This is best seen in the bread: little dots suggest the crispness of the crust.

Vermeer's most important patrons lived in Delft. The wealthy Pieter van Ruijven bought 20 paintings, including 'The kitchen maid'. The local baker owned two.

Woman reading a letter
JOHANNES VERMEER
oil on canvas, c. 1663
46.5 x 39 cm

What catches the eye in this intimate scene is the letter. The young woman has just received it. A second page lies on the table. The map on the wall may be an allusion to the sender.
Vermeer is a master at suggesting space; he plays with light and shadow. Thus the map and the chair have cast shadows on the wall, but the woman does not. The effect is to detach her from the background. Another trick is to show only part of objects such as the table, chairs and map, enough to allow one to picture the rest. Everything is reduced to the bare essentials; even the colours are limited to blue and ochre, but in an endless range of hues.

Johannes Vermeer and his Delft colleague Pieter de Hooch are the undisputed masters of the 'Dutch interior', with people – often women – in their everyday environment. The two men painted the same subjects and had an unerring feeling for light and space.

PIETER DE HOOCH 1629 - after 1683

Interior with a mother delousing her child's hair, known as 'A mother's duty'
PIETER DE HOOCH
oil on canvas, c. 1658-1660
52.5 x 61 cm

A mother is delousing her child by the light from a window. In many 17th-century households this was one of the weekly chores. This scene is only part of the painting. The interior receives the most attention: there the subtle lighting leads the viewer's eye from room to room, from the inner room with the box bed to the back of the house and the garden. The details are done meticulously: the shining floor, the Delft tiles, the paintings, the made bed and the copper bedwarmer. It is the type of neat and tidy household of which there were many in the Golden Age.

It looks as if Pieter de Hooch wanted to say something else through this domestic scene. In the 17th century combing the hair was likened to cleansing the soul. After all, bringing up children involves not only physical but spiritual care as well.

View of houses in Delft, known as 'The little street'
JOHANNES VERMEER
oil on canvas
c. 1658
54.3 x 44 cm

A woman has just scrubbed the alley beside the house; the water glistens in the gutter. She is bending over a barrel. Children are playing on the pavement in front of the house under the watchful eye of a seamstress in the doorway. It is not known whether an actual street or house in Delft is depicted here, but that is not really important. In the first place the painting is an everyday scene in a town in 17th-century Holland. It radiates calm and security.

Vermeer used muted colours with accents here and there: red and green shutters, a yellow sleeve, a blue skirt, white caps, collars and plasterwork. Through the peek into the alley Vermeer suggests depth, a device that he would have borrowed from his older colleague Pieter de Hooch. The bricks and clinkers are very roughly sketched, yet they give the impression of a wall and a paved surface.

Three women and a man in the courtyard behind a house
PIETER DE HOOCH
oil on canvas
c. 1663-1665
60 x 45.7 cm

The scene that Pieter de Hooch depicted takes place behind a house. People are having a drink in the courtyard. A woman and a man watch with interest as the woman at the table squeezes a lemon above a glass of wine. Meanwhile in the background a cauldron is being scoured.

The works by De Hooch and Vermeer show many resemblances. Both use the device of the through view. With De Hooch this is the open door in the fence. De Hooch is much more meticulous in his depiction of a house and its setting. The building materials, for example, are shown in fine detail, brick by brick. The open shutters break up the severe surface and give depth to the scene through the alternation of light and shade.

GERARD TER BORCH 1617-1681

Portrait of Helena van der Schalcke
GERARD TER BORCH
oil on panel, c. 1648
34 x 28.5 cm

Helena van der Schalcke was about two years old when she posed for Gerard ter Borch. Slightly disconcerted, she stands there in her finest dress adorned with lace and bows. The double gold chain is so large that it is held in place by ribbons. Just visible is a bit of the leading reins, a long flap on the back by which children could be restrained. Except for this detail and the pinafore she is wearing, with her fashionable clothes and wicker bag Helena looks like a small adult.

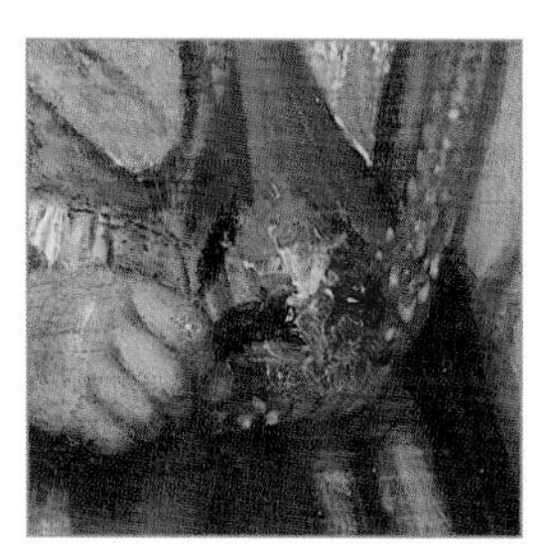

The carnation Helena is holding is seen in various portraits. It is often regarded as a religious symbol standing for the love of God and the hope of eternal life after death.

GABRIËL METSU 1629-1667

The sick child

GABRIËL METSU

oil on canvas, c. 1660

32.2 x 27.2 cm

The mother looks with concern at the child lying listlessly in her lap. Beside them is an untouched earthenware bowl of pap. The interior is simple. No paintings on the wall, but a map and a framed print – barely discernible – of the Crucifixion. Through this combination the painter may have wanted to say that the caring mother personified Christian charity. Whether or not that was his intention, it remains a moving scene painted in forceful, bright colours – red, yellow, blue and white. The surrounding grey and brownish tints are less striking. In this way Metsu focuses attention on the sick child and the kind carer.

Gabriël Metsu must have looked closely at a sick child, because hardly any depictions of sick children were made in the 17th century. More normal were paintings of mothers caring for their healthy children. They are seen breastfeeding them or removing their head lice.

JAN STEEN 1626-1679

Woman at her toilet

JAN STEEN

oil on panel, c. 1658

37 x 27.5 cm

A young woman is preparing to go to bed and takes off her stocking. Beside the bed there is a chamber pot and a dog is already lying on the pillow. This looks like an innocent scene, but on closer inspection it turns out to have various double meanings that the average viewer in the 17th century would immediately have grasped. The woman is a 'piskous', a vulgar term for a prostitute in the 17th century. This is indicated by the combination of the half full chamber pot and the red stocking ('kous' in Dutch). The word 'kous' could also mean 'woman' and a red stocking meant a whore. In this context the slippers and the dog suggest lechery. Jan Steen often gave his everyday scenes a double meaning. They were meant to instruct as well as entertain.

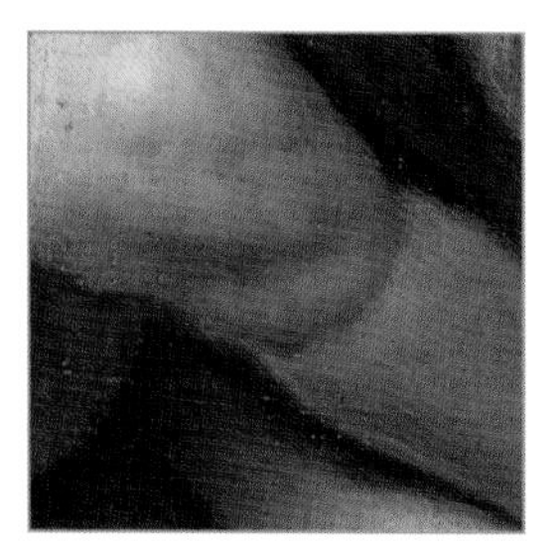

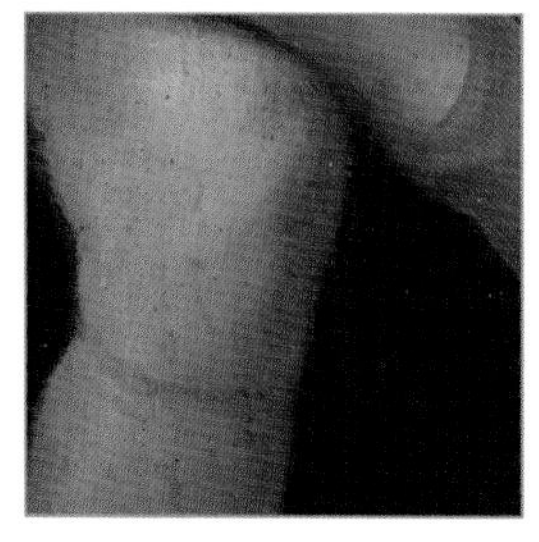

The woman is literally 'exposed'. Later ages thought this unseemly. The naked flesh and the chamber pot were painted over. The restoration in the 20th century revealed the uncensored version. The red ribbon is the garter, which has left its mark on her legs.

GERARD TER BORCH 1617-1681

Seated girl in peasant costume
GERARD TER BORCH
oil on panel, c. 1650-1660
28 x 23 cm

A young woman in peasant dress, with pinned-up plaits and red ribbons. This is what unmarried country girls looked like in the Golden Age. But this is no country girl. This is a fancy dress party, as shown by the poem she is holding. On festive occasions in the 17th century, poems were often recited by people wearing peasant dress. The girl must be the painter's half-sister, Gesina ter Borch. Her features bear a close resemblance. Gesina was used as a model quite often. Gerard ter Borch portrayed her delicately – the curls on her cheek, the pensive gaze.

Gesina ter Borch came from an artistic family. Together with her brothers, she was given drawing lessons by her father, who was himself a painter. She made hundreds of drawings and watercolours for her own enjoyment, and a single painting. This she did together with her brother Gerard, who was the only one to take up painting as a career.

The feast of St. Nicholas

JAN STEEN

oil on canvas, c. 1665-1668

82 x 70.5 cm

JAN STEEN 1626-1679

The feast of St. Nicholas or Sinterklaas is one of the most enjoyable occasions of the year in the Netherlands. Originally a Catholic celebration, it is still popular today. On the evening of 5 December children may put their shoe by the chimney, and those who have been good find a present from St. Nicholas in it. But naughty children receive the 'roe' or rod, a bundle of twigs, for a sound beating.

In this painting the 'roe' is the main motif. The small boy is pointing at it. His elder brother has been given it in his shoe and is now crying, while the boy and the maid laugh at his distress. The younger brother has received a stick for playing 'kolf', a cross between hockey and golf, and his sister has a doll and a bucket full of sweets. The other children stand singing expectantly by the chimney, knowing that is where the presents come from. The adults are thoroughly enjoying themselves. It looks as if grandmother has hidden a present behind the curtain, as a consolation for the boy in tears. The scene is entertaining and instructive at the same time. 'Those who are sweet get good things, those who are naughty the roe' says one Sinterklaas song. Jan Steen conveyed this message perfectly. He was a born storyteller and a master at arranging figures. Through a web of glances and gestures between the figures he makes clear what is going on.

Waffles and the spiced cake known as 'speculaas' are typically Dutch delicacies still made today.

The twigs of the 'roe' have faded with time.

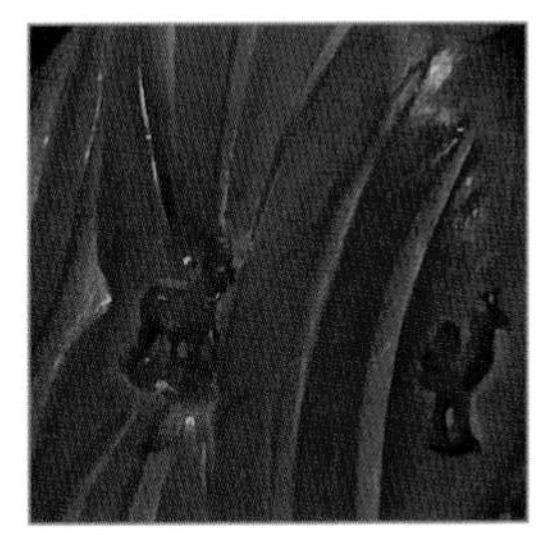

The loaf, a 'duivekater', was a type of bread eaten on special occasions.

The same faces often recur in Steen's domestic scenes. In many cases it is his own face, but members of his family are also seen. Here Steen's daughter appears as the maid.

JAN STEEN

The merry family

JAN STEEN

oil on canvas, 1668

110.5 x 141 cm

In this family everybody is having so much fun that no one notices that a small boy is following his father's example and drinking wine too. Like father, like son. This is the subject of the painting and to make this quite clear Jan Steen has also written it on the paper hanging from the chimneypiece. It says: 'Soo d' oude Songen, Soo Pypen de Jonge' (As the Old sing, So Pipe the Young). Steen has depicted this saying literally. The old sing and the young 'pipe', that is play the flute or bagpipes or smoke a pipe. The saying is also a warning to the parents to bring up their children well, for bad examples are all too easily followed. As so often with Jan Steen, the painting serves to instruct and entertain. While bad habits may be amusing, above all they are an example of what not to do.

Jan Steen had a great success with his topsy-turvy households. They made such an impression that they became proverbial, and in the 18th century the expression 'a Jan Steen household' came to be used in the Netherlands. It means a chaotic state of affairs and is still a familiar saying.

JAN VAN DE CAPPELLE 1626-1679

The home fleet saluting the state barge
JAN VAN DE CAPELLE
oil on panel, 1650
64 x 92.5 cm

Sea views were quite popular in the Golden Age, as might be expected in a sea-faring country like the Republic. This painting shows a fleet of inland ships about to depart. They are lined up one behind the other and the sails are hoisted. The State Barge fires a shot in salute and this is answered by the ship on the right. In the foreground there is a sloop full of dignitaries. The spectacle is watched from the ferry boat on the left. The imposing sky full of clouds gives a splendid effect of depth.

Jan van de Cappelle had his own yacht and must have witnessed scenes like this himself. He painted for his own pleasure and seems to have taught himself. Sea and winter views were the subjects he chose, always with the same still atmosphere and silver-grey or gold-orange tone.

Van de Capelle earned his living from a successful paint factory. He was very rich and owned a gigantic collection of paintings and drawings by artists such as Rembrandt, Rubens, Hals, Avercamp and his great model, the marine painter Simon de Vlieger.

WILLEM VAN DE VELDE II 1633-1707

A ship on the high seas caught in a storm, known as 'The gust'
WILLEM VAN DE VELDE II
oil on canvas, c. 1680
77 x 63.5 cm

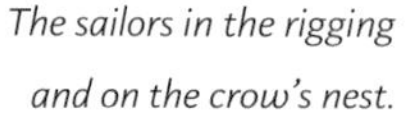

The sailors in the rigging and on the crow's nest.

Ships in storms and ships in fine weather. They show the two sides of the seaman's existence: the battle against the elements and the calm of the home port. This theme, together with the fact that the paintings are practically the same size, suggests that they were pendants.

These were favourite subjects in the Golden Age. 'The gust' shows two ships in danger. The mainmast of the merchant ship has broken and one sail has torn loose. The crew are lowering the sails. The waves are so high that the fishing boat seems to disappear in them.

The cannon shot

WILLEM VAN DE VELDE II

oil on canvas, c. 1680

78.5 x 67 cm

A greater contrast with 'The gust' could hardly be imagined. Here there is not a breath of air. The sails of the frigate hang limply and the water is faintly rimpled. It is a clear day; sunlight makes the sails stand out splendidly against the heavy gunsmoke of the shot fired in salute.

Willem van de Velde II was the most famous marine painter of his time. Like his father, Willem van de Velde I (see page 20), he was a ship portraitist in the first place. And whether the ships were in action or at anchor, no detail was forgotten. His style is remarkable: he depicted ships in fine detail, almost as in a drawing, but the sea and sky are treated more freely

Almost unrimpled water.

Father and son worked together closely. The father was the draughtsman and his son the painter. In 1672 they both entered the service of Charles II of England, from whom they each received an annual allowance of one hundred pounds, the father for drawing sea battles and the son for painting them.

PAULUS POTTER 1625-1654

Cows in the meadow near a farm

PAULUS POTTER

oil on canvas, 1653

58 x 66.5 cm

The cow is one of the most familiar features of the Dutch landscape, as it was in the Golden Age. It was a national symbol, a sign of Dutch prosperity and of the success of the dairy industry. The poet Jacob Cats wrote, 'Do not despise our Holland, we have fine cows, from which flow sweet milk and cream and butter'. The Dutch were proud of their cows. Not surprisingly, the 'cattle piece' quickly became popular after the first had been painted around 1620. Town dwellers in particular were keen to have them.

Potter's patrons moved in the highest circles. He was the outstanding painter of cows. Here he presents a sunny view of the farmer's way of life. Several cows by the farm are warming themselves in the late afternoon sun. It is milking time, given what the woman on the right is doing.

ADRIAEN VAN OSTADE 1610-1685

Peasants in an interior

ADRIAEN VAN OSTADE

oil on copper, 1661

37 x 47 cm

It is cosy at the inn. A fire crackles in the hearth and peasants have a beer together and smoke a pipe. In the foreground a man and a woman are in conversation, the rest listen. The little girl with her dish of pap only has eyes for the begging dog. An amusing scene. Van Ostade had an eye for such things.

Subtle lighting ensures that all manner of objects can be discerned in the dimly lit room: simple furniture, wooden plates and spoons, stoneware jugs and pots, a print on the wall and bird cages.
Van Ostade found his subjects in peasant life, a genre that appealed primarily to city dwellers. Initially he portrayed the raw, uncivilized side of country life, but in the middle of the century his view of the peasant became milder.

JAN VAN DER HEYDEN 1637-1712

The Nieuwezijds Voorburgwal
with the Oude Haarlemmersluis
JAN VAN DER HEYDEN
oil on panel, c. 1667-1670
44 x 57.5 cm

The bustle of activity at the Oude Haarlemmersluis produces a splendidly atmospheric view of 17th-century Amsterdam. One boat is about to leave the lock, while another loaded with sand is moored at the quay. The skipper hands a woman a bucket of sand for scouring pots and pans, as the next customer comes up the steps with her bucket. Meanwhile a man lets his dog have a swim.

This characteristic corner of Amsterdam with brick houses, gables, trees and more masts of ships beyond the lock appears to represent reality. Indeed, these are all contemporary elements, but the painter has dealt with them as he pleased. What concerned Jan van der Heyden above all was the atmosphere.

GERRIT ADRIAENSZ BERCKHEYDE 1638-1698

The bend in the Herengracht near the Nieuwe Spiegelstraat

GERRIT ADRIAENSZ BERCKHEYDE

oil on panel, 1672

40.5 x 63 cm

This part of the Herengracht is known as the Golden Bend because of the magnificent houses there. In 1672 this section of the canal was as good as finished. Only a few plots were not yet built on. The façades reveal how much the taste of the wealthy had changed. In the first half of the 17th century the canal houses were narrow and topped by gables (as in the other townscape), but now they are broad mansions with straight cornices.

Berckheyde's painting is a wonder of precision, with houses in a rhythmic pattern and strict diagonals conferring depth. The trees so characteristic of Amsterdam are missing. They were already there in 1672, but the painter left them out so that the architecture would be seen to better effect.

In the Golden Age no other city grew as rapidly as Amsterdam. This period saw the construction of the canal belt, the semi-circle of parallel canals around the centre of the city. It was built in two phases: the first from around 1610, the second from 1660.

FRANS HALS 1581-1666

'It is worth the journey to Amsterdam for that painting alone,' wrote Vincent van Gogh in 1885, when he had seen this work in the Rijksmuseum. He thought the 'orange, white and blue figure in the left corner' was especially fine; he had 'rarely seen a more divinely beautiful figure'. It was Frans Hals's style of painting that Van Gogh found so exciting. Captain Reael's Amsterdam civic guards must also have been admirers of Frans Hals. In 1633 they asked him to paint their portrait. That was unusual, because portrait commissions normally went to a fellow townsman. They did make it a condition, however, that Hals should paint the portrait in Amsterdam. Hals found travelling back and forth heavy going. Three years later, with the work still not finished, the civic guards became impatient: the portrait had to be completed within fourteen days or Hals would not be paid. Hals refused and did not get his fee of 1056 guilders.

The painting was finished by Pieter Codde, who lived in the civic guards' neighbourhood. It was not an easy task for a painter used to working with great accuracy in a small format. He tried to imitate Hals's style as best he could. Yet there is a difference: Hals's figures are alive, Codde's are rather stiffer.

The company of Captain Reijnier Reael, known as 'The meagre company'
FRANS HALS & PIETER CODDE
oil on canvas, 1637
209 x 429 cm

& PIETER CODDE 1599-1678

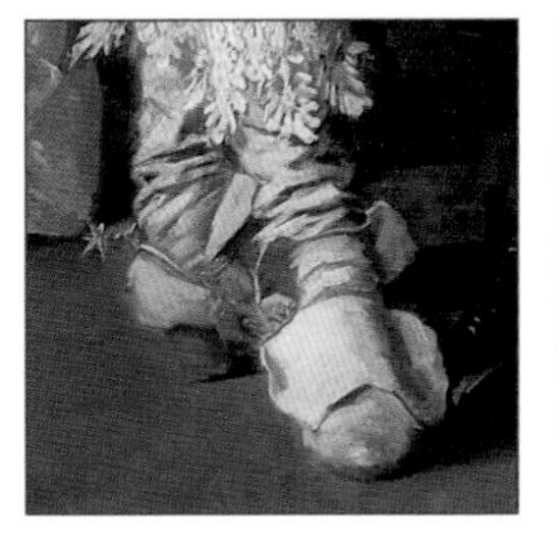

Hals

Codde

Hals

Codde

The painting was given the nickname 'The meagre company' in the 18th century because the men are rather slender, certainly when compared with the guards in other portraits.

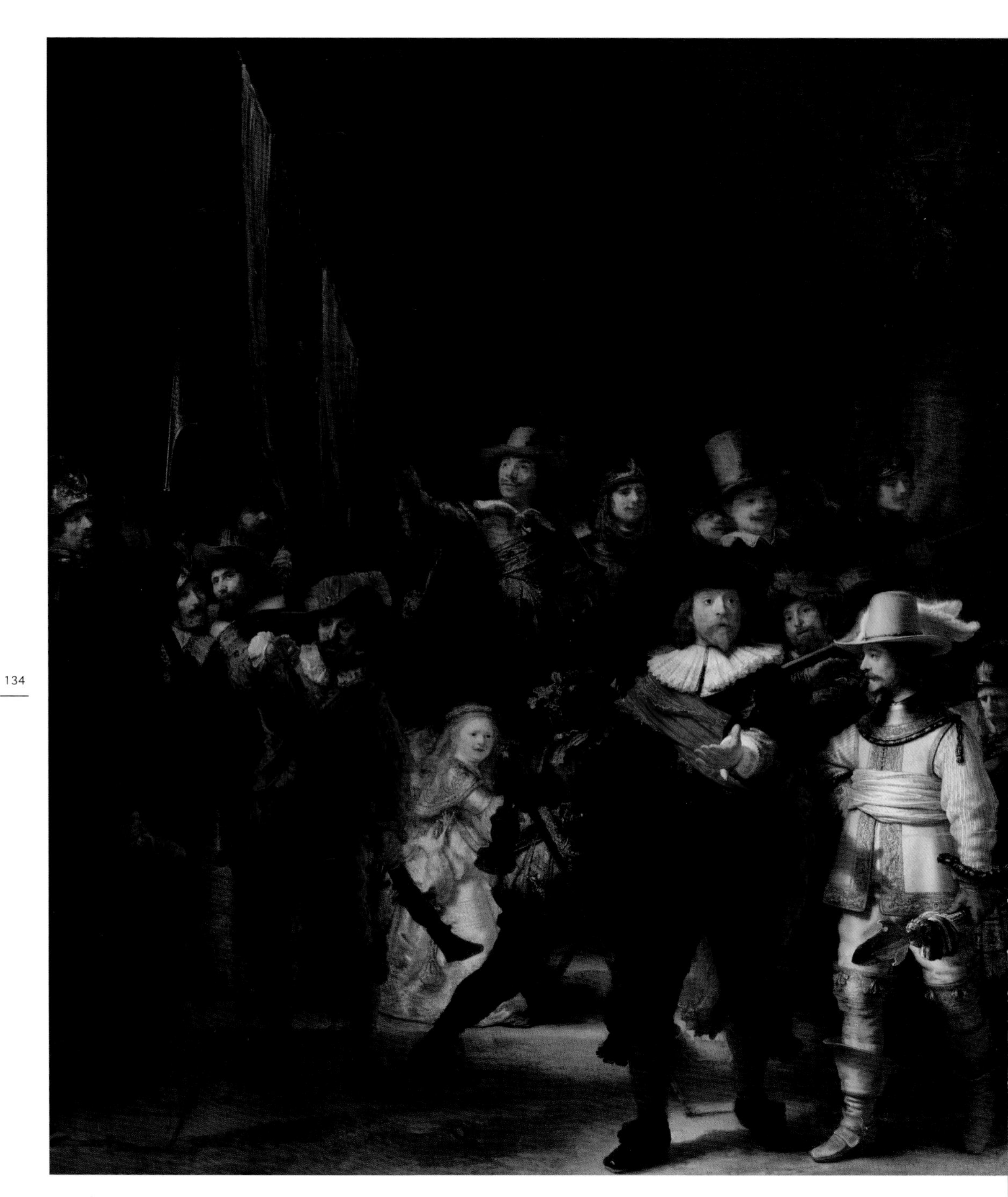

Amsterdam archers under command of Captain Frans Banninck Cocq, known as the 'Night Watch'

REMBRANDT HARMENSZ VAN RIJN

oil on canvas, 1642

379.5 x 453.5 cm

REMBRANDT

VAN RIJN 1606-1669

Frans Banninck Cocq gives the order; his mouth is slightly open.

Willem van Ruytenburch.

Loading the musket: a powder measure is put into the barrel.

The extended hand and its shadow suggest depth.

A captain gives a command and the whole company is set in motion. The ensign raises the standard, the drummer beats the drum, the guards grasp their weapons. A small girl walks between them. Rembrandt did not paint a neatly arranged portrait of civic guards in a line, but created an exciting spectacle of men in action. It is a civic guard portrait the like of which had never been seen. It became world famous.

Shown here is the company or 'vendel' of Amsterdam 'kloveniers' led by Captain Frans Banninck Cocq and Lieutenant Willem van Ruytenburch. These guards took their name from the 'klover', a firearm that had been replaced by the musket. Rembrandt gives the musket a prominent place here. Three guards demonstrate how it works. The man in red is loading; another, behind the captain, is firing, and a third, to the right of the lieutenant, blows the powder remains away.

Rembrandt indicated that the guards were 'kloveniers' through small details that are noticeable because they are caught in the light. Thus the dead bird at the girl's belt has a deeper meaning. The claw or 'klauw' was a symbol of the 'kloveniers', also known as 'klauweniers'.

Still subtler are the three crosses from the Amsterdam coat of arms in the lieutenant's yellow suit. They are incorporated into the embroidery.
'The Night Watch', as the work came to be known in the 19th century, contains the portraits of eighteen people. Their names are given on a shield high in the background. Rembrandt added the other figures to enliven the scene. The civic guards are shown in their finest clothes and with their usual weapons, as for a parade. Strong light-dark contrasts strengthen the suggestion of movement and focus attention on the portraits. The captain, in distinguished black, gives the order, and his hand comes forward. The cane, sword and gloves underline his dignity. The lieutenant stands out because of the partisan he holds; this was a weapon used only by officers. The ensign

The embroidery with the arms of Amsterdam held by a lion.

Reijer Engelen, sergeant. The halberd goes with his rank.

Blowing away the powder remains after firing.

The drummer was included at no cost.

The bird's claw is the symbol of the 'kloveniers'.

According to one of the guards 'The Night Watch' cost 1600 guilders. Another said that sixteen guards each paid about 100 guilders, some a little more, some a little less, depending on their place in the portrait.
The captain and the lieutenant would have paid separately. Only the drummer was included free of charge.
Rembrandt experienced both wealth and poverty during his life. When he married Saskia van Uylenburgh in 1634 the future looked bright. He received one commission after another and quickly became rich. The year in

has a prominent place too. There are also sergeants (two), musketeers, pikemen, men with round shields, a boy with a powder horn and a drummer, who was hired for the occasion.

'The Night Watch' was intended for the Great Hall of the Kloveniersdoelen, the civic guard's building at the corner of the Amstel and Kloveniersburgwal (now the Doelen Hotel). There it hung with five other civic guard portraits and a portrait of the managing board, all painted between 1638 and 1645 by Amsterdam's finest portraitists. In 1715 'The Night Watch' was moved to the Amsterdam town hall. The place for which it was intended turned out to be too small, so the painting was trimmed down on all sides.

Jacob Dircksen de Roy, pikeman.

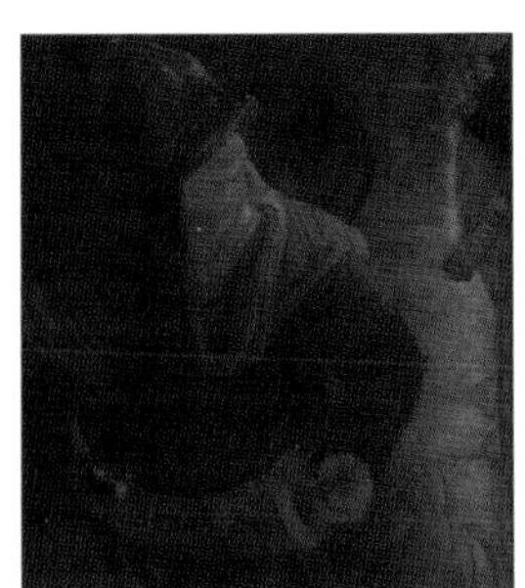

Boy with powder horn.

Fire bursts from the barrel.

The shield with the names was added later.

Copy after 'The Night Watch'

ATTRIBUTED TO **GERRIT LUNDENS**

oil on panel, c. 1655

66.5 x 85.5 cm

Lundens painted this copy for Frans Banninck Cocq. It shows 'The Night Watch' before strips were cut off on all four sides. A particularly large piece was lost on the left.

which he painted the famous 'Night Watch', 1642, ought to have been one of his best. Things turned out differently: it was the year in which Saskia died. His son Titus was less than a year old. Not long afterwards Hendrickje Stoffels became his housekeeper. In 1654 she gave birth to Rembrandt's daughter Cornelia. By then he had a great many debts and was forced to sell his possessions and to move house. In 1669 he died. He was buried in a pauper's grave in the Westerkerk in Amsterdam.

Lion resting, to the right

REMBRANDT HARMENSZ VAN RIJN

pen in brown ink on brown paper, c. 1660-1664

122 x 212 mm

The ancient beech tree

JACOB ISAACKSZ VAN RUISDAEL

etching, first state, 1650-1655

191 x 277 mm

MASTERPIECES ON PAPER

The 17th century was also a Golden Age for Dutch drawings and prints as artists explored the visual world in their drawings. Painters such as Jan van Goyen and Albert Cuyp not only made landscape drawings in preparation for their paintings but also as works of art in their own right. Without question, the most talented and versatile of the Dutch artists was Rembrandt. He proved himself an unrivalled master in not only his drawings but also in his prints of landscapes, portraits and Biblical and mythological tableaus.

The Rijksmuseum houses one of the largest and most stunning collections of prints and drawings in the world. In addition to Rembrandt's work, the collection also boasts drawings and prints by artists such as Willem Buytewech, Jacob van Ruisdael, Jan Lievens and Adriaen van Ostade. Highlights from the collections will be displayed alternately in a series of presentations in hall 13.

Italian nobleman

WILLEM PIETERSZ BUYTEWECH

etching, 1615

191 x 72 mm

WORK IN PROGRESS

The main building of the Rijksmuseum is currently undergoing extensive renovations to ensure it meets all the requirements of a modern museum. More than 7000 objects, soon to be displayed in eighty different halls, will cover the period from the late Middle Ages to present day. Paintings, sculptures, historical objects and the decorative arts covering more than six centuries of art and history will be on display in a building that is fit for the 21st century.

By the end of the 19th century, the architect Pierre Cuypers had created a veritable *Gesamtkunstwerk* with his masterful Rijksmuseum. Ornaments on the outer walls depict important events in Dutch art history, a simple lay-out structured around two courtyards makes it easy for visitors to find their way around the museum, and vivid wall decorations in the halls of the museum find resonance in the transparent and easily navigable building. The aim when renovating this rich artistic heritage is to re-establish Cuypers' ideas in order that visitors may enjoy the most beautiful historical objects from the entire Rijksmuseum collection.

Cuypers' original ornaments in the Hall of Fame have been reconstructed and re-fitted.

Design by Wilmotte & Associés for a hall to house the 18th century collection.

OBJECTS AND THEIR NUMBERS

All the objects in the Rijksmuseum have a unique number. Please refer to these numbers when inquiring about the objects in this guide. They are given here arranged by page.

p. 10 Banquet in celebration of the Treaty of Münster
BARTHOLOMEUS VAN DER HELST
SK-C-2

p. 12 Andries de Graeff
ARTUS QUELLINUS
BK-18305

p. 13 Amsterdam town hall on Dam Square
GERRIT ADRIAENSZ BERCKHEYDE
SK-A-34

p. 14 The four continents pay homage to Amsterdam
ARTUS QUELLINUS
BK-AM-51-3

p. 16 Model ship William Rex
C. MOESMAN
NG-MC-651

p. 18 Counter decoration of the English man-of-war Royal Charles
NG-MC-239

p. 19 Michiel de Ruyter goblet
NICOLAES LOOCKEMANS
NG-NM-9659

p. 20 Battle of Terheide
WILLEM VAN DE VELDE I
SK-A-1365

p. 21 Ewer and basin
JOHANNES LUTMA
BK-NM-10244

p. 22 Model for the tomb of Maarten Tromp
ROMBOUT VERHULST
after a design by Jacob van Campen
BK-NM-4352

p. 23 Portrait of Michiel Adriaensz de Ruyter
ROMBOUT VERHULST
BK-NM-13150

p. 24 Fishing for souls
ADRIAEN PIETERSZ VAN DE VENNE
SK-A-447

p. 26 Portrait of Maurits, Prince of Orange
MICHIEL JANSZ VAN MIEREVELD
SK-A-255

p. 27 Princes Maurits and Frederik Hendrik at the Valkenburg horse fair
ADRIAEN PIETERSZ VAN DE VENNE
SK-A-676

p. 28 Execution sword
NG-NM-4245;
Johan van Oldenbarnevelt's walking-stick
NG-NM-548

p. 29 Hugo de Groot's bookchest
NG-KOG-1208

p. 30 Nassau tunic
NG-KOG-42

p. 31 Assembly of the States General
DIRCK VAN DELEN
SK-C-1350

p. 32 Prince's Day
JAN STEEN
SK-A-384

p. 33 The bodies of the De Witt brothers
attributed to JAN DE BAEN
SK-A-15

p. 34 Amsterdam as the centre of world trade
PIETER ISAACSZ
SK-A-4947

p. 36 Portraits of Jan Valckenburgh and Dina Lems
DANIËL VERTANGEN
SK-A-4969/4970

p. 37 VOC base at Hougly in Bengal
HENDRIK VAN SCHUYLENBURG
SK-A-4282

p. 38 Kendi
NG-1977-172

p. 39 Cradle
BK-1966-48

p. 40 The Cnoll family
JACOB JANSZ COEMAN
SK-A-4062

p. 41 View of Olinda, Brazil
FRANS POST
SK-A-742

p. 44 The dolls house of Petronella Oortman
BK-NM-1010

p. 48 The dolls house of Petronella Dunois
BK-14656

p. 50 Interior with women beside a linen chest
PIETER DE HOOCH
SK-C-1191

p. 51 Galant conversation, known as 'The paternal admonition'
GERARD TER BORCH
SK-A-404

p. 52 Dignified couples courting
WILLEM BUYTEWECH
SK-A-3038

p. 53 The tailor's workshop
QUIRINGH VAN BREKELENKAM
SK-C-112

p. 54 Basin and ewer with Diana and Actaeon, and Diana and Callisto
PAULUS VAN VIANEN
BK-16089

p. 56 The Adoration of the shepherds
PAULUS VAN VIANEN
BK-1979-101

p. 57 The Resurrection of Christ
PAULUS VAN VIANEN
BK-1959-14

p. 58 Basin and ewer
ADAM VAN VIANEN
BK-AM-17A/B

p. 59 Ewer
ADAM VAN VIANEN
BK-1976-75

p. 60 Two salt-cellars
JOHANNES LUTMA
BK-1960-13

p. 61 Dish
JOHANNES LUTMA
BK-NM-13258;
Portrait of Johannes Lutma
REMBRANDT HARMENSZ VAN RIJN
RP-P-OB-549

p. 62 Bacchus discovers Ariadne on Naxos
ADRIAEN DE VRIES
BK-14692

p. 63 Triton blowing a conch
ADRIAEN DE VRIES
BK-C-1997-2

p. 64 Plate
BK-NM-3133;
Inkstand
BK-NM-12400-79

p. 65 Bust of Prince William III of Orange as king of Great Britain
Delftware factory DE METALE POT
BK-NM-12400-93;
Bust of Mary II Stuart
Delftware factory DE GRIEKSCHE A
BK-1960-11

p. 66 Shoe
BK-1957-11;
Violin
BK-NM-12400-91

p. 67 Teapot
Delftware factory
HET MORIAENSHOOFT
BK-16535

p. 68 Parts of a tile wall from the Water Gallery at Hampton Court
Delftware factory DE GRIEKSCHE A
BK-KOG-1681 and BK-KOG-2567

p. 69 Flower holder in the form of a stacked obelisk
Delftware factory DE METALE POT
BK-14852

p. 70 Cabinet
attributed to JAN VAN MEKEREN
BK-1964-12

p. 72 Console table with the four seasons
BK-14980;
Two guéridons
BK-1972-157-A/B

p. 73 A pelican and other birds near a pool, known as 'The floating feather'
MELCHIOR D'HONDECOETER
SK-A-175

p. 76 Winter landscape with ice skaters
HENDRICK AVERCAMP
SK-A-1718

p. 78 The cattle ferry
ESAIAS VAN DE VELDE
SK-A-1293

p. 79 Still life with flagon, glass, jug and bridle
JOHANNES TORRENTIUS
SK-A-2813

p. 80 Portrait of a man with ring and touchstone
WERNER VAN DEN VALCKERT
SK-A-3920

p. 81 Bust of Vincent Jacobsz Coster
HENDRICK DE KEYSER
BK-NM-11452

p. 82 The fête champêtre
DIRCK HALS
SK-A-1796

p. 83 The serenade
JUDITH LEYSTER
SK-A-2326

p. 84 Wedding portrait of Isaac Abrahamsz Massa and Beatrix van der Laen
FRANS HALS
SK-A-133

p. 86 The merry drinker
FRANS HALS
SK-A-135

p. 87 Portrait of a girl dressed in blue
JOHANNES VERSPRONCK
SK-A-3064

p. 88 Still life with cheeses
FLORIS VAN DIJCK
SK-A-4821;
Still life with turkey pie
PIETER CLAESZ
SK-A-4646

p. 89 Still life with gilt goblet
WILLEM CLAESZ HEDA
SK-A-4830

p. 90 Interior of the St. Odulphus Church in Assendelft
PIETER SAENREDAM
SK-C-217

p. 91 The former city hall in Amsterdam
PIETER SAENREDAM
SK-C-1409

p. 92 Self-portrait at an early age
REMBRANDT HARMENSZ VAN RIJN
SK-A-4691

p. 93 Self-portrait as the apostle Paul
REMBRANDT HARMENSZ VAN RIJN
SK-A-4050

p. 94 Jeremia lamenting the destruction of Jerusalem
REMBRANDT HARMENSZ VAN RIJN
SK-A-3276

p. 95 Portrait of Johannes Wtenbogaert
REMBRANDT HARMENSZ VAN RIJN
SK-A-4885

p. 96 Portrait of Maria Trip
REMBRANDT HARMENSZ VAN RIJN
SK-C-597

p. 97 Portrait of Andries Bicker
BARTHOLOMEUS VAN DER HELST
SK-A-146;
Portrait of Gerard Bicker
BARTHOLOMEUS VAN DER HELST
SK-A-147

p. 98 River view by moonlight
AERT VAN DER NEER
SK-A-3245

p. 99 Landscape with two oaks
JAN VAN GOYEN
SK-A-123

p. 100 Italian landscape with draughtsman
JAN BOTH
SK-C-109

p. 102 River landscape with riders
AELBERT CUYP
SK-A-4118

p. 103 The windmill at Wijk bij Duurstede
JACOB VAN RUISDAEL
SK-C-211

p. 104 Festoon of fruits and flowers
JAN DAVIDSZ DE HEEM
SK-A-138

p. 105 Still life with silver jug
WILLEM KALF
SK-A-199

p. 106 Isaac and Rebecca, known as 'The Jewish bride'
REMBRANDT HARMENSZ VAN RIJN
SK-C-216

p. 108 The syndics of the Amsterdam drapers' guild
REMBRANDT HARMENSZ VAN RIJN
SK-C-6

p. 112 The milkmaid
JOHANNES VERMEER
SK-A-2344

p. 114 Woman reading a letter
JOHANNES VERMEER
SK-C-251

p. 115 Interior with a mother delousing her child's hair, known as 'A mother's duty'
PIETER DE HOOCH
SK-C-149

p. 116 View of houses in Delft, known as 'The little street'
JOHANNES VERMEER
SK-A-2860

p. 117 Three women and a man in the courtyard behind a house
PIETER DE HOOCH
SK-C-150

p. 118 Portrait of Helena van der Schalcke
GERARD TER BORCH
SK-A-1786

p. 119 The sick child
GABRIËL METSU
SK-A-3059

p. 120 Woman at her toilet
JAN STEEN
SK-A-4052

p. 121 Seated girl in peasant costume
GERARD TER BORCH
SK-A-4038

p. 122 The feast of St. Nicholas
JAN STEEN
SK-A-385

p. 124 The merry family
JAN STEEN
SK-C-229

p. 125 The home fleet saluting the state barge
JAN VAN DE CAPELLE
SK-A-453

p. 126 A ship on the high seas caught in a storm, known as 'The gust'
WILLEM VAN DE VELDE II
SK-A-1848

p. 127 The cannon shot
WILLEM VAN DE VELDE II
SK-C-244

p. 128 Cows in the meadow near a farm
PAULUS POTTER
SK-A-711

p. 129 Peasants in an interior
ADRIAEN VAN OSTADE
SK-C-200

p. 130 The Nieuwezijds Voorburgwal with the Oude Haarlemmersluis, Amsterdam
JAN VAN DER HEYDEN
SK-A-154

p. 131 The bend in the Herengracht near the Nieuwe Spiegelstraat, Amsterdam
GERRIT ADRIAENSZ BERCKHEYDE
SK-A-4750

p. 132 The company of Captain Reynier Reael known as 'The meagre company'
FRANS HALS & PIETER CODDE
SK-C-374

p. 134 Amsterdam archers under command of Captain Frans Banninck Cocq, known as the 'Night Watch'
REMBRANDT HARMENSZ VAN RIJN
SK-C-5

p. 137 Copy after 'The Night Watch' attributed to GERRIT LUNDENS
SK-C-1453

p. 138 Lion resting, to the right
REMBRANDT HARMENSZ VAN RIJN
RP-T-1901-A-4524;
The ancient beech tree
JACOB ISAACKSZ VAN RUISDAEL
RP-P-OB-4860

p. 139 Italian nobleman
WILLEM PIETERSZ BUYTEWECH
RP-P-1982-1

INFORMATION

Rijksmuseum Amsterdam
Address for visitors:
Jan Luijkenstraat 1
Postal address:
Postbus 74888
1070 DN Amsterdam
Latest information:
T +31 20 6747 000
F +31 20 6747 001
E info@rijksmuseum.nl
I www.rijksmuseum.nl

Opening times:
The Rijksmuseum is open daily from 9am to 6pm and on Fridays till 8.30pm. Closed on 1 January.

How to get there:
Tram 2 + 5 (Hobbemastraat stop)
Tram 6, 7 + 10 (Spiegelgracht stop)
Tram 12 (Concertgebouw stop)

Photography:
Photography is not permitted in the Rijksmuseum.

Mobile telephones:
The use of mobile telephones is not permitted.

Text:
This guide was written by the Department of Education & Information: Marleen Dominicus-Van Soest, with the assistance of Ineke Jungschleger.

Translation:
John Rudge, Amsterdam

Photography:
The Rijksmuseum Department of Photography and other bodies listed in the captions.
To these should be added for the photograph on pages 14-15: Stichting Koninklijk Paleis te Amsterdam, photo: Jan Detwig.

Design:
Studio Jas, Amsterdam

Language switch:
Anja Nerrings, Lalleweer

Floor plan:
Irma Boom Office, Amsterdam

Printing:
Kunstdrukkerij Mercurius, Westzaan

WITH THANKS TO:

PHILIPS

BankGiroLoterij

ING